How to Raise Great Kids in
a Generation of Assholes

How to Raise
Great Kids in
a Generation
of Assholes

LIZ PARKINSON

LIONCREST
PUBLISHING

HOW TO RAISE GREAT KIDS IN A GENERATION OF ASSHOLES
*Cut through the BS of Parenting to Give Your
Kids the Tools They Need to Be Awesome*

ISBN   978-1-61961-571-7 *Paperback*
         978-1-61961-572-4 *Ebook*

This book is dedicated to all parents who want better for their kids and are willing to do what it takes to see it through, and to Florence's mom who in her perfect proper English accent said to me, "You should write a book about parenting."

Contents

Grab a Glass of Wine and Settle In

There are days when I wake up and miss the "old me." I miss the time when I could sleep in late, answer to no one, and be concerned about only my own agenda for the day, even if all it included was shaving my legs and watching four consecutive seasons of *Sex and the City*. But having kids, even just one, blows that whole idea completely to hell! Your body, your time, and your very existence suddenly belong to someone else.

I used to feel guilty about having those feelings and think I was failing as a mother. I'd silently wonder if maybe I wasn't cut out for motherhood. I know there are thousands of women who struggle with fertility issues and would die for being able to wake up every morning knowing they're a mom. But I got over it. Three kids in and I've begun to realize that it's OK to miss the former single me. I know there's nothing wrong with having days when I just don't feel like being a mom. And I've even made peace, more importantly, with the fact that my kids will be assholes at times, and that I don't have to like them every single day.

We all know kids can be assholes, and it's our job as parents to let them know when they are. We have to help and guide them in changing their negative behavior, which won't always be an easy thing to do.

One evening, I decided to take my kids, who were aged ten, seven, and three at the time, to the local ice-cream store for an after-dinner treat. They were superexcited and so was I. Who doesn't love ice cream?

We entered the store and the kids walked up to the young girl at the counter, who couldn't have been more than sixteen herself. She had a look on her face that screamed, "I'd rather be anywhere else but here!"

They each ordered an ice-cream cone, and off she went to get everyone's favorite flavor. When she returned, she handed them their cones one by one. Each kid took their ice-cream cone without saying a word. Not one word. I waited for them to thank the girl—to say something to express their appreciation to her for making their cones. You could tell she was waiting, too, because she paused a moment after handing over each one. Her face said exactly what I was thinking: *What a bunch of fucking brats!* My kids just started eating their ice cream.

I felt my face start to flush from rage and embarrassment. For all the thousands of times I'd reminded them to be polite, kicked them under the table, gave them the stare of death from across the room, or placed a not-so-gentle hand on their shoulder, they just stood there like three ungrateful brats licking away. I quickly thanked the girl and made our escape.

As soon as we were out the door, they stood waiting for me to open the car doors. Instead, one by one, I took their ice-cream cones and threw them in the trash. The three of them stared at me, wide-eyed and confused, and my youngest burst into tears. To add insult to the injury, a mother walked by just then in horror, assuming I was fucking insane.

After my youngest caught his breath, and his blue face from the tantrum returned to normal, I asked them if they knew why I'd tossed their cones. They looked at one another perplexed, the boys scratching their heads and shrugging their shoulders for dramatic effect.

Then my oldest said, "I don't think we said thank you."

Bingo!

TEACHABLE MOMENTS

I could have chosen to let the whole thing go, or I could've told the kids when we got in the car that I was disappointed they hadn't remembered to say thank you. But I would've wasted an opportunity to teach my children a lesson they'd never forget. As harsh as it may have seemed to them, I took advantage of a powerful teachable moment. Never again, hopefully, will they forget to say thank you, thanks to the shock value of what I'd done. Of course, part of me felt bad, but the other part really wanted to drive home the point. They got in the car and were upset, but they got over it.

Taking advantage of a teachable moment is something I refer to throughout this book. It's natural for us parents to want to protect our children and not upset them, but there are times when I think it's necessary for making a point. If you can get past the feeling that you're hurting your kids—which you're not; you're simply upsetting them in the moment—then you can take advantage of those situations and make a lasting impression on your kids.

The incident with the ice-cream cones was profound, especially for my youngest child. He's still a work in progress as far as manners go, but the older two are quick to say thank you now. Too often, parents pass over teachable moments. They're busy and don't want to take the time to deal with things as they happen, but it's precisely in those situations that you have the opportunity to make an impact on your children and their behavior.

Taking advantage of a bold teaching moment also means following through consistently. You may not do anything as extreme as throwing an ice-cream cone in the trash bin, but you don't want to become the kind of parent who always warns but never follows through. If you brush bad behavior under the rug when it happens, kids will start to fall back into their old ways. Creating habits takes time, and following through requires discipline. Whether positively or negatively, all behavior needs reinforcing. When my kids say thank you appropriately, I always let them know I appreciate it, and when they don't, I correct them. Either way, I follow through. Eventually, all the hard work will pay off, and thank you will become a natural part of their vocabulary.

You want to avoid getting into situations in which you have to backpedal. You don't want to end up dealing with something when your kids are older that you should have dealt with when they were young. I always say I'd rather pick up my kids from the principal's office than from juvenile hall.

Habits are a lot harder to break once behavior is established. Taking advantage of teachable moments when your kids are young will pay big dividends when they get older.

Unless you maintain consistency throughout your parenting, you'll end up with an asshole kid. And let's face it, we all know an asshole kid. Whether it's a friend's child or a friend of one of your children, they are out there. And the truth is, it's usually not their fault.

I know there are parents who think that when their child has reached the age of thirteen or fourteen, their job is done. If that's what you think, then you need to pull your head out of your ass. Adolescence is a critical time when kids start to form ideas about real-life issues. If you're not there to guide them and answer their questions, they'll establish their own opinions from wherever they can find them. This is the time in their lives when you get to see the fruits of your labor from the first fourteen years applied to real-life shit that matters.

THE KIDS ARE WATCHING

Parenting requires an evolving set of skills. You're probably not going to want to parent like your parents did, and I bet your parents didn't parent like their parents. The things kids have to deal with today weren't even dreamed of when I was growing up. Even though I don't feel my childhood was all that long ago, my daughter's life is drastically different than mine was. The world is changing fast, and parents need to develop new skills all the time. I want to be clear here: I'm no expert. In fact, at least once a day I feel I have failed as a mother somehow, but I've learned a lot from being a parent to my three kids. I'll share with you everything I've found that works and creates awesome kids.

Kids are truly fascinating creatures. Prior to being a mother, I worked with obese children. I'm a certified personal trainer and also have certifications in nutrition for athletes. Working with the overweight kids was a tricky and emotional experience. They were young and unfortunately given the wrong set of tools to start out with in their lives. They faced an uphill battle to lose weight. It's hard enough to learn basic life skills when you're young, but when you add weight loss into the mix, it becomes a monumental task. Kids just want to be kids. Having to lose weight makes them feel like they're being punished. About 90 percent of the time, it's the fault of the parents, who usually are extremely overweight themselves. They set their children up for failure at a young age because the kids will follow whatever their parents do and eat what they are given or what they see their parents eating. And then the kids are expected to deal with growing up along with all the shit that comes from being overweight.

Working with children opened my eyes to how much children watch and mimic adults. I saw that if children had asshole parents, they'd repeat the same asshole behavior they saw their parents do. It got me thinking about how I wanted to parent when I had kids. I realized how important it is to be a positive role model for children and that until I could get my own shit together, I should keep investing in birth control!

You've already met my three kids from the ice-cream debacle: my daughter Soleil is thirteen now, Everest is nine, and Kesler is five. My husband, Aaron, and I run an online health and fitness company, which is a full-time eighty-hour-a-week job. Fortunately, we both work from home, which has allowed me to be both an entrepreneur and a full-time mom.

Our business is dedicated to helping clients achieve a healthy lifestyle by making one small change per week. We do this by reinforcing healthy habits every day. Our work is about lifting people up, supporting them, and celebrating their small victories so that they continue to succeed. Each small victory adds up to big change. We used the same method of positive reinforcement that worked so well with our kids, who liked being told "You did great!" or "I'm so proud of you."

My husband and I grew up in very different types of families. I grew up in a conservative, well-to-do household with strict rules and curfews. The rules in my house were nonnegotiable, but that didn't stop me from trying to bend them as much as I could. My dad was a business owner who was raised during the Depression, and he had a say in everything that went on in our house.

Education was extremely important to both my parents, so my sister and I were fortunate enough to go to private school. I loved my parents' theory on private school. In their minds, we were being sent to school with "good" kids from "good" families. In reality, we were just a bunch of little assholes who had more access to all of the things our parents thought they were sheltering us from!

My mom was of the belief that everything should be made from scratch, including bread. Very few things were store bought. I didn't even go to McDonald's until I was twelve years old.

Aaron's family was the complete opposite. He came from a more casual household. He had the cool house, the "let's drink beer at Aaron's house because his dad is OK with it" house. It was the house I always wanted growing up. His dad was a food distributor, so he grew up with closets full of potato chips, sour keys, and gummy bears. He even had a soda machine in his bedroom! He had a lot more freedom than I did and was given more self-determination, which is a topic I go into later in the book. Because of our diverse backgrounds, Aaron and I often talked about the kind of parents we wanted to be. We decided to take the parts we loved from both our sets of parents and incorporate them into how we wanted to parent together.

Aaron and I work fucking hard at being good parents. It frustrates me to see parents coming up with excuses for why their kids are misbehaving and refusing to take responsibility for their parenting methods, or lack thereof. They prefer to shift the blame to something external when in reality, they created their own nightmare by allowing their children to rule the home.

Our kids are great, which is not to say they're perfect. Kids are never perfect and are always a work in progress. We put a lot of work into establishing ground rules and boundaries from the beginning, and as a result, less is required now as the kids get older. I think a lot of parents aren't willing to put the time in to create a positive foundation. They fluff off bad behavior because they're too busy, too uninterested, or too into their smartphones, friends, image, or job to give a shit. These are the same parents who then blame society, teachers, and the school system for not doing the job they should be doing.

We've had lots of positive results with our children from

taking a firm stance from the start. I hope this book helps you establish a baseline of good behavior with your kids and to not be afraid to take advantage of teachable moments whenever they may happen.

TIRED? ME, TOO!

Parenting is a fucking grind from the very beginning. It doesn't have an on-off switch. It's an all-day, everyday effort from the time the kids wake up in the morning to the time they go to bed at night. It's exhausting. Most days are a blur of making lunches, carpooling, homework, sports practice, bath time, bedtime stories, and maybe, if you're lucky, getting a moment to yourself. The really bad days have the added bonus of frustration, pity parties, and the occasional "this is bullshit" under your breath as you fold the umpteenth load of laundry. But I can't imagine my life without children. I love being a mom, although the reality is, nobody wants to tell you how tough it is. I find that over the years, I've become the friend who's not afraid to say that parenting can suck.

Before my first baby was born, my sister said to me, "Don't expect to do anything fabulous for the first eight weeks. If you get up every day, manage to have a shower, and your baby is clean, fed, and happy, then that's a huge success!" I loved her for that honesty. I'd often be lucky to just brush my hair. Nobody tells you the truth about having a newborn because they don't want to create any disillusions about how wonderful it is to have a baby. The same is true for parenting.

Each stage of parenting is different. Now my husband and I have a foot in several phases. We have a young boy in elementary school, another boy in middle school, and a daughter who's entering adolescence. None of these stages is any easier than the other. Of course, I no longer have to help my daughter get dressed or cut up her food, but I do have to deal with emotional heartbreak, social media, and the many other challenges of being a teenager. And I'd much rather deal with a bump on the head or a temper tantrum any day than a girl's broken heart!

Parents have a tendency to think that the next phase of parenting will be better than the one they're in, but the truth is, each stage has its own set of obstacles and challenges. Let that sink in for a moment. It's never going to be easy being a parent. It'll require all your energy at every age. Even now that I am forty, I know my mom still worries about me, my health, my family, and my finances. Remember that if your eyes are always on the next stage hoping it'll be easier than the one you're in, you'll miss having fun with your children and establishing good behavior in the present. When you're in the middle of crying babies, the grass may look greener for the parent who has a teenager, but you'll discover soon enough that teenagers, too, have their issues that need your attention. Then you'll look back and remember the glorious days when your kids couldn't talk!

SOME GROUND RULES

Raising a child who's not an asshole boils down to some basic ground rules:

☞ *Don't be lazy.* Always follow through. I know it isn't always convenient, but neither is your period, and you still find time to change your tampon. Being consistent when teaching appropriate behavior is critical.

☞ *Remind your kids about their manners every day.* Correct them when they're doing something inappropriate. If a thank-you is required and doesn't happen, point it out to your child. And when it does happen, also remember to thank them for using their manners.

☞ *Turn bad behavior into teachable moments.* Making mistakes is how we grow. Failure is just a stepping-stone to doing it better the next time. Embrace those moments when things go wrong as an opportunity for a teachable moment.

☞ *Embrace the day-to-day grind.* Know that parenting is exhausting work and that at the end of the day, all you'll want to do is to fall into bed. Remember that even though it feels like a grind, what you're doing is going to create fabulous kids. And if at the end of the day you need a glass of wine to celebrate another successful day of not killing your children, then do it!

A fabulous kid doesn't mean a perfect child. Kids learn and grow daily and need to be cut some slack. That said, a fabulous kid to me is one who's well behaved, particularly when not at home. You should expect your kid to challenge you at home. That's what kids do. It's when they go to someone else's house that you want to hear rave reviews about how great and well behaved they were. That to me says you're doing your job because they know how to act in public and be around other people.

A fabulous kid is also one who's a confident member of the family. His or her opinion is valued. I want my children to feel their voice is heard no matter what their age. That's how they'll develop positive self-worth. You may not want to hear all 156 names of the Pokémon characters, but listening to what is important to your kid in the moment is what establishes trust for more serious conversations to come.

Growing up is a learning process. If you establish good behavior when your children are young, it will hopefully provide a foundation for the rest of their lives.

In this book, my husband, Aaron, and I share what's worked for us. Our hope is that it'll help you know what to expect as you move through the different stages of parenting and give you the skills to create fabulous kids.

CHAPTER 1

Cut the Supermom Bullshit

Being a parent is fucking tiring. Always has been, always will be. But it's especially exhausting in the era of Pinterest-inspired everything. Here's why it's OK to give yourself a break.

The supermom syndrome is the number one, most unfortunate development in modern parenting. I believe the "supermom" was created through social media and has influenced way too many women on how they think a mother should be.

A supermom works full time. Her house is always clean and

tidy. Her kids are perfectly put together and have all the latest and greatest toys every child has got to have. She's a PTA mom, a chauffeur, and able to whip up twenty-four perfectly coiffed cupcakes for the school fund-raiser.

Supermoms don't have an off switch. They don't ever say no when asked to volunteer, and they're constantly trying to one-up other supermoms to show them they have their shit together. Oh my God, it's exhausting and unhealthy! I know because I was one.

One spring, my daughter Soleil's class was having an Easter party. Typically, parents sign up to bring something to the party. In previous years, one mother, who was a professional cake decorator, always brought cupcakes, and they were amazing—flowers made from fondant, animal faces, Christmas trees. You name it and this woman could create it on a cupcake. This time, I decided I wanted to beat her to the list and bring cupcakes myself. I thought, *How hard could it be?*

I managed to sign the list before she did, which turned out to be an insult for her. She couldn't believe someone else would make cupcakes.

I had the idea to make cupcakes with little bunny toppers on them, like I'd seen on Pinterest. The bunny's head is made of a cotton ball stuck on a toothpick so it won't touch the cupcake, with ears and whiskers painted on. I had to make thirty-six of them.

It was 1:00 a.m. and the cupcakes had to be done the next day. I sat at my kitchen table putting them together while everybody else was sleeping. I was exhausted because I'd worked all day and had a newborn asleep upstairs. There I was, painting whiskers on bunnies in the middle of the night, convinced that my cupcakes were going to be the greatest of all time. Deep down, though, I knew I had already fucked myself. In three hours, my baby would need to be fed, which would leave me only two hours of sleep after that. It's pretty hard to appear perfect with huge black craters under your eyes.

What the fuck was I doing? How did I get to this place of being alone in the middle of the night with thirty-six bunnies glaring at me? It took every bit of energy I had not to squash their little faces. Who was this all for? The truth was, I already knew the answer. I was making cupcakes to show all the other mothers how great I was! I was showing them that I, too, could make fabulous cupcakes with a job and three kids. The professional cake decorator had only one kid after all. Wouldn't I look awesome when I brought those bunny cupcakes to school?

This was my defining aha Pinterest moment, and it truly was life changing. Although it sounds dramatic, it instantly made me rethink my priorities.

I could've just as easily made cupcakes with sprinkles on top, and the kids would have been just as happy, but I was looking for recognition from the other moms. Instead of making something simple, enjoying the evening with my kids, and getting a good night's sleep, I'd become obsessed with impressing everyone, and it was making me cranky and miserable.

I quit cold turkey, and it was hard because I had become addicted to the challenge. But I didn't want to try and be a supermom anymore and place unrealistic expectations on myself just so I could prove I had my shit together, which I clearly did not. I'd become exactly the kind of mom I would have judged on the playground as being fake or pretentious, yet there I was, striving for the same thing. I just wanted to enjoy being a mom again.

HOW PINTEREST HAS MADE PARENTHOOD SUCK

I love Pinterest, don't get me wrong. It's a great source for so many amazing things, from diet plans and recipes to inspirational quotes and instructions for making incredible things. Where else could I have found out how to make nunchakus out of noodle floats for my son's Ninja Turtle birthday pool party? I made twenty-four of them!

When Pinterest first came out, I'd surf around the site, pin cool stuff, and hang out there all day. Pinterest is like Martha Stewart on crack. I think it was the turning point in making motherhood an ultracompetitive sport. First, it started out being about what I could do for my children, and then it became what I could do to show off to other mothers.

It's not easy to make the things you see on Pinterest within any kind of normal budget. Many of the party ideas come from professional party planners and cost accordingly. It's even worse when your kids get involved. I made the mistake of giving my daughter a Pinterest account. She wanted me to make things she saw that she liked. She'd find something she wanted for a party, and I'd have to figure out how to create it without spending the next month's income.

I also blame Pinterest for the one-upmanship of kids' birthday parties. All of a sudden, parties became about what you could do bigger and better than the last one and less about the kids. You can give kids a box of water guns, let them loose in the backyard, and they'll have a blast. It's normal to want your kids to have a special experience on their birthday, but you have to ask yourself whom you're really doing it for and why.

I wasn't done with my competitiveness. It came out in other ways when we lived for three years in the Caribbean on a small affluent island known for its banking industry and financial institutions, a place where the average person wouldn't shop at Walmart or Target even if there'd been one.

Owning a fitness company, I pretty much live in workout gear and jeans, yet I started dressing like the other moms and making sure my hair was perfect when I picked up the kids, which was even more exhausting. It's not that I ever went to the school looking like a fucking homeless person, but doing hair, makeup, and designer clothing in ninety-five-degree heat is no fun. I squashed this bullshit quickly. My kids didn't care how I looked when I got them from school, and I wasn't comfortable in the clothes I was wearing. It wasn't me, so I stopped pretending and went back to wearing jeans and a T-shirt or my workout gear if I came from the gym. I stopped giving a fuck about people's opinions that didn't matter in my life.

I also used to volunteer for everything. I felt I should be in my kids' classrooms as much as possible. Every time there was a field trip, I'd go. Every time there was a need for a driver, I'd offer. It got to the point where my husband said I was being ridiculous. He loved that I wanted to help out but said my volunteering was becoming a full-time job. I knew he was right and that there had to be a balance. What

I discovered after I stopped all the volunteering was that my kids were more excited on those occasions I did visit their classrooms. It became something special, which it hadn't been when I was there all the time. The last thing I wanted was to become Pam's mom.

Pam (not her real name) was a girl I went to high school with from grade eight through twelve. When I first met Pam, I thought she was supersweet, quiet, smart, and an extremely fast talker. Her mom was a fixture in our school. She was a PTA mom, volunteered for everything, and was always on campus. At first, I thought how lucky Pam was to have her mom spend so much time helping in our classroom. And in the beginning, Pam also seemed to like the fact that her mom was known by everyone in the school. But as the years wore on, Pam gradually began to resent her mom's presence—she was always there, always around, always in her business. It was too much. By grade twelve, the tension between them was brutal. It's no wonder that when Pam began applying to universities, she decided to move across Canada to attend school. It was not because she fucking loved poutine!

During my supermom days when I was running my company, volunteering in the kids' classrooms, and creating special projects, I slept only a few hours a night so that I could get everything done. Once, I even spent an entire night making safari animal cookies with multiple colors of icing for a school bake sale. Being a supermom affected my mental state, the way I treated my husband, and how I was with the kids. I was supposedly doing everything for my children, but when it came to parenting, I was impatient and had no time. I would find myself snapping and sneaking moments to get away from the family. Frankly, I had become a total bitch.

At the end of the day, kids are simply happy to see their mom. They don't care what she's wearing. It doesn't matter to them whether the cupcakes have bunnies with whiskers or sprinkles. They just want to spend time with you. When they're older, they aren't going to look back and remember the freakin' bunnies on their cupcakes. They're going to remember the time you spent together, the quality time when you laughed, got silly, and were just loving in the moment.

All that pressure to keep up appearances and prove you're at the same level as everybody else will never work anyway. There'll always be someone who one-ups you and looks more put together than you do. What I've learned over time is that we're all dealing with the same shit and pressure as mothers. It's just that some moms are better at hiding their crazy shit than others. So be perfectly imperfect and get over being a supermom. Sometimes you just have to say, "Fuck it," for the sake of your sanity. Take it from me, you'll be a much happier person when you do.

SUPERMOMS CREATE ASSHOLE KIDS

When I was being a supermom, I set a high bar. I was constantly trying to outdo myself with each class event, celebration, and birthday party. After a while, my kids started to expect nothing less. If I only had time to do something basic, they'd say to me, "Is that *all* you're going to do, Mom?"

It wasn't that they were intentionally being assholes. It was my fault because I'd set such a high standard; they thought it was the norm. Anything less seemed like it wasn't enough. Inadvertently, I'd created unreal expectations in them. They were disappointed even when I did try to make more of an effort.

I started innocently enough, thinking I was doing amazing things for my kids even though in reality, I was doing it for my own recognition. As a consequence, I ended up creating unrealistic expectations in my children.

I have the luxury of working from home, but mothers with nine-to-five jobs or single moms who don't have the budget for a Pinterest party, for example, are at a disadvantage. Kids will compare them to other mothers, which is nobody's fault but our own. If we think we're better than others, our kids will pick up on it and do the same thing. They'll think their mothers are more creative and care more than other moms do.

Getting too involved in your kid's school projects is another way to create an asshole kid. In striving to prove I was the best mom in the school, I wanted moms, teachers, and other kids to perceive my kids as geniuses. I wanted every one of my kids' projects to be creative and perfect, with every pompom or piece of construction paper perfectly placed. This got to the point where I was actually completing my kids' class projects in the name of helping them get it done. If you don't think that teachers can see right through that shit, then you're kidding yourself. Teachers can always tell when it's happening. They know the level of work to expect from an eight- or nine-year-old child. You need to let go of your OCD and let your kids cut and paste things on crooked and color outside the lines. It's their journey, not yours, which is not to say, of course, that you shouldn't encourage your kids to do their best work.

I was 100 percent guilty of this myself. Even though it comes from a place of good intention, interfering too much encourages and enables asshole behavior in two ways: first, it forces kids to be competitive with their classmates instead of focusing on doing great work, and second, kids start to expect that you'll do their projects for them. Then when you tell them to do something on their own, they'll feel like you're letting them down when, in fact, they should've been doing the work themselves in the first place.

I realized that I hadn't been empowering my kids when I

helped them so much with their projects. While it's natural as parents to want to help out and guide our kids, the work needs to be theirs. Kids have to learn what hard work is. Even more importantly, their work should never be about you and your competition with other mothers!

A TEACHABLE MOMENT

Once, I heard my son being critical of his friend Michael's mom and saying that she was lazy. I asked him why he thought she was lazy, and his response was that she never made anything cool for their class and only brought juice boxes for parties. I stopped him on the spot to take advantage of the teachable moment. I pointed out to Everest that Michael's mother has a job and goes to work every day. It took her an hour to drive home at night.

I told him how great it was that Michael's mom was able to find the time to go to his classroom and read to the kids, and that she sent cookies to school on Michael's birthday.

Unless we explain those things to our kids, they won't appreciate the full story. They'll focus on only the fact that Michael's mom doesn't make amazing cupcakes, which, of course, is no big deal. Michael's mom is still a great mom.

HOW TO OVERCOME THE PRESSURE TO BE AN ÜBER-PARENT

I quit being a supermom cold turkey, which may not be right for everyone. It worked for me, even though it was tough on the kids at first. They noticed the difference and understandably missed all the amazing things I used to make and do for them. They had been proud of my creations, but once I realized that I wasn't doing it for them, it was never the same. I went into a "you're the coolest mom ever" withdrawal. Hearing that from your kids becomes addictive.

I explained to my kids what was going on. Of course, I didn't say I was stopping because I was becoming a bad mom. They wouldn't have been able to understand that. I told them that I was spending too much time and energy on little things and not enough time on the things that really mattered—like being with them, getting my work done, and getting some sleep. By my stepping back, I said, we'd be able to spend more time together doing the things we loved instead of my stressing out about cupcake toppers. Then they understood.

Maybe I went too far stopping all at once. They weren't just disappointed that I wasn't bringing great projects into their classrooms anymore; they also missed the cooking and baking we used to do together. Soon, though, I gradually began adding activities back in. I didn't want them to feel like they were being punished. I still wanted to spend time with them in the kitchen and do arts and craft projects together. I just didn't want it to be about my competition with other mothers anymore.

Instead of obsessing about being a perfect mom, I went back to making cookies with my kids that weren't perfect and having fun doing it. I didn't care if they were expertly decorated, although it did take practice to overcome my fucking control issues. I had to learn to get over all the gobs of icing and sprinkles and just have a good time making cookies. And that's how it should be.

If you take nothing else from this chapter, it's this: learn how to say no and mean it. As a mom with school-aged kids, there will always be something to volunteer for. When I was asked to volunteer, I used to say something like, "I'm sorry, but I'm too busy." That inevitably led to the next question, "Why are you too busy?" I quickly learned a more powerful reply: "I'm sorry, but it's not a priority for me right now." That phrase is a fucking atomic bomb to other mothers. There's no comeback when you put it like that. It took confidence for me to say it and mean it, but when I did, people understood that I meant no. There wasn't anything more to talk about. No one was going to argue with me about my priorities. Learn that reply and use it!

Perfect Dad Pictures

I've got a buddy whom I've known for a long time. He's what you'd call a guy's guy. He's all about money, boozing it up, and golfing. I'm sure you know the type.

He got married and had kids because he felt like he had to. Lots of guys think it's what they're supposed to do even if they're not really cut out for it. There's nothing wrong with feeling that way; it's just that guys don't acknowledge it. They go ahead and have kids anyway and end up being crappy dads and causing a bunch of unnecessary harm when they shouldn't have gotten married and had kids in the first place.

My friend was like that. They had their first kid and had nothing but drama. Then they had the second one. Then the third one. They just kept going even though things were getting progressively worse. What a dumbass!

Then I watched as he constantly put his needs before everybody else's, even on family days. Half the time, he'd be drinking at the bar with his buddies, talking about work. Yet amazingly enough, once a month a bunch of pictures of him doing all these awesome things with his kids would show up on Facebook.

Of course, it's great that he went out and spent time with his kids, but he took a once-a-month event, packaged it up, and threw it up on a Facebook page. He wanted to appear like he was an amazing dad, which only made things worse. All his buddies knew what he was really like, so he just ended up looking like a total douche.

Don't be that guy. Schedule your time if you have to. Take care of your wife and be a real dad. It will save you a lot of stress in the future.

CHAPTER 2

Parenting Is a Team Sport

A family can look so many different ways today. And that's awesome. But whether you're in a traditional family, a same-sex parenting situation, or single, you gotta have some help.

I'll never forget my daughter Soleil's twelfth birthday. She wanted a slumber party with her friends to celebrate. We were living in the Caribbean at the time, which meant it was a pool party, too. After swimming, the girls wanted to go to the beach to play Pokémon Go.

The island we lived on is a very safe place. It's small with little crime and not much danger. I always felt comfortable with my kids riding their bikes around the neighborhood or walking up the street on their own to a friend's house. It's the kind of place where the one local homeless guy is a celebrity. The last time I saw him, he'd been picked up by a bachelor party and was hanging out in the back of a limo drinking bourbon. He was having a more fabulous Saturday night than I was!

To get to the beach, the girls—there were six of them—had to cross a fairly busy road. When they asked my permission, I figured with the six of them, it was safe to let them go on their own. As they were getting ready to leave, my husband, Aaron, walked in and asked where the girls were going.

I told him they were going to the beach for a Pokémon hunt. "No, they're not!" he said.

I explained to him that I'd already told the girls they could go, but he was uncomfortable with the plan. I think it was probably due to the fact that the average twelve-year-old girl these days looks like she's at least sixteen or eighteen, and there was a small, crazy local bar on the beach where they were headed.

What happened was unusual for us. Aaron and I had made a decision as parents to never argue in front of our children, but this time, we got into a back-and-forth in front of the girls about why they could or couldn't go to the beach. We never yell at each other, even in our most heated discussions, so we weren't shouting, but it was definitely an argument.

Unfortunately, we weren't paying attention to the fact that we looked like assholes in front of our daughter and her friends. Soleil was totally embarrassed and stood there hoping we'd shut up.

In the end, we compromised and let the girls go to the beach, and as it had been my idea, I went along to check on them now and then but not to watch their every move. I took my book, walked across the road with the girls, and settled nearby to keep an eye on things.

If I'd been in my daughter's shoes at age twelve, I would have been mortified seeing my parents argue in front of my friends. It was only later, after she told us how embarrassing it had been for her, that we realize what jerks we'd been.

It's always been our goal as parents to be a united front. Even if we don't like what the other one is saying, we don't disagree when the kids are there. When we began parenting, we watched what other parents did, talked about the arguments we'd seen our parents have, and decided never to be divided in front of our kids. No one likes to witness their parents, or anyone else for that matter, having a disagreement, but on Soleil's birthday, we got caught up in the moment and were more concerned about being right than listening to each other. In the end, the situation gave us an opportunity to come together and realign about upcoming changes, given Soleil was almost a teenager. But that was no excuse for what happened. It would have been much better for everyone concerned if we'd been able to talk things over privately, not to mention that we seriously took our coolness level in the eyes of our daughter down a huge notch.

WHY COPARENTING IS SO IMPORTANT FOR KIDS

When kids see that you and your partner are not a united front, they'll try to take advantage of the situation and manipulate you. We've all done that ourselves as kids.

I remember growing up knowing when to go to my mom and when to go to my dad. I, like all kids, knew who was the weaker parent in any given situation. Kids pay attention to what their parents say and learn to play their parents off each other. We like to think our kids won't do that, but they all do. Kids are only interested in getting the answer they want and will go to the parent they think will give it to them.

I had strict parents, but my dad was always less strict than my mom when it came to doing adventurous things. I was somewhat of a tomboy, and whenever I wanted to play sports or do something like water ski at the lake with my friends, I'd go to him. I knew he'd see it as an adventure while my mom would worry that I'd get hurt or want to know if other parents would be around. Depending on the situation, I chose which parent to go to for permission. If parents aren't both on the same page, that's what happens. And they'll probably never get the full story of what's really going on. They'll get the part about going water-skiing but not that there'll be underage drinking going on. The problematic part of the plan gets conveniently left out.

Kids are more perceptive than we like to think. They pick up on conversations even when we think they're not listening. It happens even more as kids get older. I've heard my two eldest repeat things I said in a conversation that I didn't have a clue they were listening to. Their ears had become satellite dishes. It's not uncommon when I am discussing something with Aaron that my son Everest will ask from the next room, "Who are you guys talking about?" or "Sorry, I missed that last part; what happened?"

When parents divorce or separate, parenting as a united front becomes more difficult. It presents a situation with problems of its own. Not to generalize, many divorced parents often don't get along for a reason, which is why the marriage didn't work. When two people have difficulties communicating due to anger or hurt feelings, it can be even more challenging when the topic has to do with their children. Also, parents may change their parenting styles after a divorce and do things differently than when they were a couple.

It's important for divorced parents to try to put their children first, despite their personal pain, which I know is easier said than done. We all have stories from friends and family where this was simply not possible, and it became a nightmare for everyone concerned.

My sister divorced six years ago and has two girls. It took her and her ex-husband a long time before they were able to communicate about their children. Whenever they had an important issue to deal with, they'd do it over e-mail as it was the only way they could communicate without being hurtful with each other. What I admired about my sister was that despite her own pain, she never talked down about the girls' dad in front of them. She encouraged their communication with him when he moved out of the country. She listened when they had stories about their dad because she recognized his importance in their lives. Eventually, her hurt subsided enough to gradually open up more lines of communication with her ex. It didn't happen overnight, but in the end, the process was a success because of their commitment to the mental well-being of their daughters.

If divorced parents can come together on the big issues, children will benefit and feel that their parents are on the same page. It gave my nieces a sense of calm, knowing their parents were communicating.

Coparenting isn't always an easy journey, but I think it goes without saying that you should strive to put your kids first in all circumstances.

AVOID RAISING AN ASSHOLE KID

It bears repeating: kids are perceptive. They sense who the weaker parent is and will prey on that parent like a lion chasing a deer. They'll go for the kill to get what they want.

Don't ever allow your children to manipulate you. They're always going to put their best case forward so they get what they want. If you aren't diligent as a parent and ask questions about what your kids are up to and where they're going, you'll come across as a pushover. Don't avoid asking the tough ones: Will there be drinking? Who will be there? What are the parents' phone numbers? If they can't or won't answer those questions, then it's a major red flag. What's key is to always be prepared for the answer.

You'll end up creating animosity if you don't coparent and talk things over with your partner, and you'll look like an asshole if your coparent disagrees with you and overrides your decisions. Then children get disgruntled, react to the lack of communication, and start taking advantage of the situation. A cycle of negativity sets in between you and your kids.

Your kid, too, risks becoming an asshole and even a bully. You can end up creating a kid who's always looking for an opportunity for personal gain, whether good or bad. Then manipulation becomes a habit. A kid who learns to manipulate will manipulate everyone, not just his or her parents, and that is definitely an asshole trait.

I hate to use the word *bully* because I think it's overused. Parents can be too quick to point out that the kid who said an unkind word to their child is a bully. But don't get me wrong, I fully understand the difference between being unkind and being a bully. We've dealt with an emotional bully with one of our kids, and there'll likely be more.

In every kid's life, there will be moments when he or she will be unkind. My kids have said mean things to other kids in a heated moment, if they're angry or there's no sharing going on. Even as adults, when we get mad, we say unkind things to one another. We can all be assholes and aim to hurt with our words, but that doesn't classify us, or our kids, as a bully. Kids have an amazing asshole ability to know and say exactly what will hurt, but they're just being brutally honest and haven't developed the social filters yet to control their language.

I define a bully as someone who's continually unkind and aggressive or uses emotional power plays to alienate kids. As parents, we tend to react defensively and label any child a bully. That can be unfair unless it's an ongoing problem.

At the same time, whenever your kid is mean, it's never acceptable. You need to stop that shit as soon as you see or hear it. You don't want to create a bully by not stepping in and helping your child to see the bigger picture and the consequences of his or her behavior. We can become mama bears who've been poked when our kids are picked on or if they're labeled a bully too quickly. Deal with it in the moment so that it doesn't escalate. Kids are in a continual process of learning, so take advantage of it!

COPARENTING TIPS

☞ Have an honest conversation with your partner about the type of parents you want to be *before* having kids. Understand that this can change and evolve as you grow as parents.

None of us can help but draw from our childhood experiences when we become parents, but unless you discuss your experience with your partner, the two of you will deal with your children in different ways. You should discuss the pros and cons of what you both grew up with in order to find out what kind of parents you want to be.

You'll set yourself up for failure if you don't have those discussions prior to having kids or, at the latest, when they're young.

You won't become perfect parents overnight. A lot of parenting is trial and error. In fact, you probably won't become the parent you want to be until you're in the middle of it.

☞ Parenting with your partner is an ongoing conversation.

Aaron and I have seen our parenting change and evolve as our children have gotten older. As new situations arise, new ways of parenting are needed. The key is to make sure that the foundation of your parenting stays the same.

Just like your kids are a work in progress, so is parenting.

☞ It's OK to disagree as parents.

You and your partner are not going to agree on everything.

Discuss the reasons why and come to a compromise.

☞ Help your children understand the basis of your decisions, as appropriate for their age.

It's important that your child understands why you've come to the conclusions you have.

Here's an example:

Soleil is a preteen who wants to become more independent, which is great, but she's not ready for everything. The old saying, she's "twelve going on twenty" is alive and well in our house.

We live near a reservoir. One day, Soleil and her three friends wanted to walk there, swim, and sunbathe. My husband and I discussed it in another room and came to the conclusion that she could go, with conditions. When we told Soleil, we made sure she understood *our* concerns—not dad's concerns or mom's concerns.

We explained the compromises and our reasoning—how far out they could swim depending on how strong a swimmer her friends were, when they had to be back home and why, and so on. If we had decided that they couldn't go, we would have told them why as well. We don't like saying yes or no without giving reasons. However, not all decisions require a lot of detail: "Mom, can I jump off the roof onto the trampoline?" "Um, no, that would be dangerous."

I want my children to understand that the decisions we make on their behalf are not meant to make them unhappy; they are not quick, unconsidered decisions. I want them to realize that there is a process behind our saying yes or no.

☞ It's OK for your kids to be mad.

It's unlikely your children will agree with every decision you make—or, more likely, nine times out of ten, your kids will momentarily hate you. They'll get angry, and that's OK. We forget that there's nothing wrong with kids being mad at their parents. In any given week, at least one of my kids—if not all three—will be mad at me. And sometimes it'll be all three at once. They may not like me every moment of the day, but that's what their friends are for.

I want to make it very clear that I'm not my children's friend. Say it yourself: "I am not my child's friend."

It's your *job* from the moment you have kids to raise them as good people. They'll love and respect you for it if you're fair, honest, and unconditionally loving. Too many parents want to be best friends with their kids and are unaware how it's become more important to them than parenting. I am not here to wear matching outfits with my daughter or buy alcohol for my sons. If that is what you think parenting is, then it's time you grew up.

THE IMPORTANCE OF KEEPING YOUR ADULT RELATIONSHIP STRONG

Having a solid, positive relationship with your partner adds to the strength of your parenting. When your children see you and your partner being respectful and loving with each other, it teaches them how to be respectful and loving. They learn from seeing their parents listen to each other's opinions and speak to each other in a loving, kind way. It's as much my husband's job to set a good example for our boys on how to treat a woman as it is for him to show our daughter what standard she should be looking for when she grows up.

If your children see you treating each other poorly, they'll adopt the same behavior. It's not hard to see when kids have picked up habits and language from their parents.

This story illustrates my point:

We have friends who divorced a couple of years ago. It was a messy, angry divorce for lots of unpleasant reasons. It took them a year to separate homes so the kids were constantly in an environment of arguing. It got to the point that we'd bring the kids over to our house to give them a break.

My son Everest was friends with the couple's son. Once, when the boys were playing together, I heard their son say to Everest, "My dad says all women are stupid."

Either his dad had said it to him directly, or he had heard his dad say it to his mother. Either way, it will affect how he grows up and his views of women. That's how learned behavior begins. Whether you believe it or not, this mentality morphs into objectifying women. It fuels young men into believing they're better than girls, which leads to the belief that girls should not be valued. Eventually, that leads to thinking it's OK to rape an unconscious girl because she made the mistake of drinking too much at a party. Sound harsh? It is fucking harsh, and it happens every day, so think about it.

Creating an *environment of respect* for one another will lead to behavior that carries on outside of the home. Respect, like anything else, has to be taught, and it starts with parents who are being respectful with each other.

Being affectionate with each other is also important. I want my children to know that I love their dad. Hugging and kissing him and being playful with him in front of them is how they'll see what a healthy relationship looks like. It shows them what is loving, positive touch and what is acceptable.

One of the best things we've ever done as parents and for maintaining our relationship is to have *date night* every Friday night without fail. My kids know it; our friends know it; my family knows it. Ever since my oldest child was about a year old, Aaron and I go out every Friday night, whether we're tired and don't feel like it or not.

Sometimes stuff comes up and we can't make it on Friday, so we'll go instead on Saturday. We never let a week go by without taking time for the two of us. It can be as simple as going out and grabbing burgers, or it can be a fancy dinner. Sometimes we join friends for an event. Whatever it is, we get out of the house and away from the kids for a few hours as a couple.

When you've got kids, it can be easy to forget that you started out as two people who couldn't get enough of each other. Adding little people to the mix, which, needless to say, causes lots of distraction and chaos, shouldn't take away from the fact that you were a couple who wanted to spend all your time together.

Date night gives you the space to take a step back and enjoy each other's company, reconnect, and reflect. Even if you spend the whole time talking about your kids and what a terrible week it's been, that's OK. You're regrouping and getting back on the same page. If anything difficult happened during the week, you can discuss it. Or you can just laugh and have a good time. A date doesn't have to be anything more than time for the two of you to be together. It will make you better parents in the long run. Some of our best conversations have happened over sharing a burger and a beer.

The same goes for taking parent vacations without the kids, even if it's for only a night or two. I still want grown-up vacations with too much eating, too much drinking, spending a lot of time naked, and sleeping all day. It's better than Disneyland any day. And it's healthy for you, and healthy for the kids to miss you. Of course, we love being with our kids, and that includes learning how to miss them.

Whenever Aaron and I go away, even for the weekend, we can't wait to see the kids when we get back. Typically, Aaron starts to miss them before I do, but that's because I primarily organize their lives. A break from them is a break from their scheduling, which is practically a full-time job in itself.

Time away makes you appreciate how much you love your kids. They, too, have a great time being away from us, but when we're home again, there's nothing better than hearing our kids say how much they missed us. The first time I left Soleil, she was four months old. We were headed to a business conference in Mexico, and I left her with my sister for five days. I cried all the way to the airport and felt intense guilt for leaving. But one margarita in and a naked swim in the ocean with my husband, it was exactly the thing I needed for my soul. Five days of couple behavior made me a better mother when I returned home. So, let go of the guilt around leaving your kids and take care of yourself for a change. You're absolutely allowed.

The Currency of Relationships

One of my friends was having trouble in his marriage and started staying at our house because it was getting too tough at home. One night in front of the campfire, I asked him what was going on.

He told me how stressful things were in his business and marriage on top of having a new kid. He wasn't sure he'd be able to keep it all together. So I started asking him questions about his life, what his weeks were like, and things like that.

I asked him when was the last time he'd gone out on a date with his wife. It'd been two years. I couldn't believe that shit. Two fricking years!

I asked him the last time he'd let his wife sleep in. He didn't even know!

And, no surprise, he said they hadn't slept together since they'd gotten pregnant with their second child. She's not attracted to you? No shit, Sherlock. She's too tired and knows you don't give a fuck.

Here I am with this guy who hadn't slept with his wife for a year, hadn't let her sleep in once, hadn't ever changed a diaper, and he was asking me why his relationship was falling apart!

That's when I explained to him what Liz and I call the currency of relationships, which is something we talk about a lot in our house. There's no money in a relationship. If you have a typical relationship, the money is everybody's money. But there are currencies in a relationship.

One currency is sleep, which is why every single week we both get to sleep in. Personal time is a currency—getting to go to the gym, going for a drive, reading a book, fluffing around on Facebook, whatever you want to do. Sex is a currency. Sometimes you've got to make time for it just to blow off steam. We learned a long time ago that if you don't schedule sex, it'll never happen. So we schedule date night. We schedule sex. We schedule our free time.

What does this have to do with parenting? Everything. If you're happy, your kids feel it and they are happy. If you're a good example of how to parent, they'll see it and duplicate it. It's simple, but so many people don't get it.

CHAPTER 3

Turn Off Your Propeller

There's so much helicopter parenting today. Your kid is not a glass egg. Here's why you're doing your kid a disservice and how to cut the shit.

Helicopter parenting didn't exist when I was a kid, which is not to say there weren't overprotective parents when I grew up. There were, but now things have reached a new level of extreme. We're doing our children an injustice by being so overprotective. Kids need to explore, jump, play, and climb, and with these adventures come some injuries. It's just part of it all.

My oldest son, Everest, is small for his age and knows it. We didn't want his size to be an issue for him or to lead to a lack of self-confidence. He'll grow more for sure, but he'll probably always be one of the smallest kids in his class.

To help build Everest's confidence, we thought martial arts would be good. We liked the mixed martial arts platform because it allows kids to figure out which martial art they prefer before getting pigeonholed into one of them.

One of Everest's weekly classes was jiu-jitsu, which is a strategic sport. It involves a lot of rolling around on the mat to get your opponent into various holds in order to gain a dominant position.

To me the idea of jiu-jitsu is terrifying. If somebody were on top of me all the time, trying to gain position, I'd get extremely anxious, but Everest took a shine to it. He's patient and likes to think things through.

My husband, Aaron, used to take Everest to his jiu-jitsu class and would take advantage of the time to get in a workout himself while he was there. One afternoon, he wasn't able to take Everest to class, so I took him instead. It was the day of the test for a belt in jiu-jitsu.

I sat with the other moms and dads who'd come to watch.

Then it was Everest's turn. His opponent stood across from him, and suddenly I panicked. The kid was probably a full head and shoulders taller than Everest. I was looking around at the other parents, wondering if they thought that the kid looked about thirty years old, too. I asked myself how could the sensei put these two boys together. There was no way Everest could win. I was sure he was going to get hurt and I started to break out in a cold sweat.

They started to roll, and sure enough, the boy got on top of Everest and dominated him. My heart was pounding. I felt claustrophobic. Silently, I kept repeating, *Oh shit! Oh shit!* I couldn't sit still. I jumped up and was ready to break up the boys. I wanted to get that kid off my son.

Then the miraculous happened. Everest flipped the kid, got on top of him, and took position. He ended up tapping out the bigger kid, meaning he got the bigger kid to give up.

I'm sure that I was the loudest, most obnoxious mother in the room at the time. I cheered and danced and was so excited because Everest had pulled off such an amazing maneuver, not realizing that was how it was supposed to be done; I didn't understand that jiu-jitsu is all about patience and waiting for the right moment to act.

The overprotective, oversensitive mother in me wanted to

jump in and save my son because I felt he was in danger. In reality, he was in control the whole time.

LET YOUR KID FAIL

Helicopter parenting suffocates children. Too many parents prevent their kids from figuring out things on their own, which robs them of the ability to make their own decisions, good or bad.

A helicopter parent is unable to separate himself or herself from his or her child's world.

You have to learn to let go. You have to let kids figure shit out on their own sometimes. You don't need to go on every field trip, drive to every event, and host every party as a way to overcome the fear that something terrible may happen to your kid. Of course, we all want to protect our children from harm, but we also have to let them have their own experiences in life, including making mistakes.

Good parenting never comes from a place of fear. Failure is essential for growth; it's a stepping-stone to learning. If your children never fail, how can they move forward? Even if you know things won't turn out the way your kids want them to, it's to their benefit if you let them make choices for themselves. Later, you can help them understand why their decisions failed if that's what happened. Then, hopefully, they'll learn not to repeat the same mistake. Even a rat can be taught not to touch the same hot plate twice.

It's not hard to understand why parents are so protective these days. The world has changed a lot since we grew up. We often think we're facing more serious issues today, but I sometimes wonder if that's really the case. Maybe we're just more aware of what's going on these days due to mass communication and social media. I'm sure thirty years ago there were sexual predators and drug addicts, but perhaps parents weren't as aware of them then. Today, we have Fox News, CNN, and Facebook, which unfortunately make every incident viral. Yes, we need to be extra careful but not to the extent that we fail to empower our children or help them learn to make decisions on their own.

The bottom line is, your kid will become an asshole if he or she doesn't have coping skills or any experience dealing with disappointment and failure.

I have a close friend who's about ten years older than me. We met when I was pregnant with Soleil, taking an exercise class together. She was a prime example of a helicopter parent before the term even existed.

My friend's son, whom I love to bits, is one of the most

dependent, helpless twenty-two-year-olds I've ever met. His mother always did everything for him. In fact, she still does. It would not surprise me at all if I were to find out that he still sleeps in her bed (which, by the way, he did until he was twelve years old)! She never allowed him to forge his own path growing up.

When my friend's son was a university student, he once wrote a paper that his professor didn't like and got a C. He'd always been a good student, so it was unusual for him to get poor grades. Immediately, his mother got on the phone and called the professor and berated him for giving her son such a low grade. She called his freakin' teacher at twenty-two years of age! And the worst part was, he expected her to.

If my mother had done that when I was twenty-two, I would have lost my fucking mind. I would have died of embarrassment, dug myself a grave in the backyard, and crawled right in.

My friend was teaching her son the same thing she'd taught him since he was a little boy: mommy is here to save you. You can do no wrong because mommy will fix it. Mommy will make things better.

I still think of her son as a little boy, even though he's in his twenties, because he still acts like one. He lives at home. His mom cooks for him, cleans his room, does his laundry, and even packs his lunch for school. I pity the woman who marries him. He is essentially a huge pussy. Unfortunately, the damage is done. My friend created an asshole who can't deal with disappointment. He doesn't know how to fail, and he doesn't know how to pick himself up and try again.

I've told my kids that if they're OK with having an average grade, then they can do average work, but they can't complain to me about it. If they're not happy with a grade, it's their responsibility to work harder. And I find that they do work harder because they don't like having a bad grade. It's not that I'm unavailable to help them with their homework if they need it. I'm more than happy to sit down and explain a problem if they are having trouble figuring it out, but I want them to understand that the level of effort they put in will equal the results. There are no excuses.

LEARNING TO PLAY ALONE

I love to play with my kids. It's probably the one thing I feel most guilty about not having enough time for. But when we do play, we have a blast. We color, bake, and do things outside. But there comes a time in the day when the kids have to play by themselves, whether it's with one another or on their own. If you feel that you have to entertain and occupy your kids 24-7, then you're a helicopter parent. Although I appreciate the effort, I totally disagree with that approach. I believe it's good for kids to be able to sit quietly and do something on their own, to create their own fun and use their creativity. Only children tend to play better by themselves, I think, simply because they don't have siblings around.

When I find my kids walking aimlessly around the house looking for something to do, I encourage them to figure it out on their own. If they're constantly looking to me for stimulation, they won't know how to think for themselves, learn to use their time wisely, or appreciate having alone time. It can be scary for children not to know how to be by themselves or rely on their own resources.

I wasn't like that as a kid. I wanted to be constantly entertained and surrounded by friends all the time. What killed me the most was Sundays.

Sunday was family day in our house, and we were not allowed to have any friends over. The problem was, we never did anything together as a family. My mom cleaned, my dad was usually in the garden, and my sister played with Barbie dolls in her room. Not only could we not have friends over, but we couldn't go over to anyone else's house either. Needless to say, I generally wandered around on Sundays completely pissed at everyone. It didn't help when my mom would say things like, "If you're bored, you can always help me clean."

I love it when my daughter goes to her room and crawls into bed with a book for an hour, or when my boys disconnect from technology, grab their Lego blocks, and build something marvelous. Sometimes they'll ask me for suggestions about what to build, which I give them, but I don't sit there and build with them. They don't need my constant input. If you're always providing the entertainment, you'll never raise an independent child.

Left to their own creativity, kids will produce amazing things.

BUSY PARENTS ARE GOOD FOR KIDS

I'm a busy mom. I have a full-time job running a company with my husband. In addition, I have coaching clients, and because we have a fitness business, I also have to devote time to keeping fit. I like to joke with Aaron, saying, "Why couldn't you have started a fucking doughnut company? You had to pick fitness?" In short, I simply don't have time to hover over my children 24-7.

There are mothers, however, who do have time to hover. Their children become their whole world. They can't separate themselves from their children's lives. That's often what fuels a helicopter parent. If you have nothing to occupy your time other than your children, the situation can become toxic. Your kids need to learn to think and form opinions independently.

Remember my friend Pam's mom (see chapter 1)? Because her mom was always around, Pam felt she could never fully express herself for fear of being judged by her mother. She always held herself back from getting in there and experiencing what all teenagers want: to have a bit of healthy dangerous fun. Pam couldn't let loose, couldn't be wild, and—God forbid!—stand up to her mother. That's how a child's passion is suffocated.

Hovering parents only let their kids experience the good or the bad within certain limits. They create a box to protect their children from danger, criticism, or having too much fun. If you're always around to prevent failure and to tell your child how great she is, then she'll be devastated when she steps onto a soccer field, for example, and fails. Being told by her friends that she's not the best player on the team or that she has work to do to be able to play the game will not be the worst thing in the world. It'll teach your child humility. And if she isn't as good as she thinks she is, you have an excellent opportunity on your hands for a teachable moment. You can talk things over with your kid and find out what it is she wants to do about it. If she wants to get better at soccer, then she'll have to practice. If she doesn't care, then she doesn't need to worry about what the other kids think and just play and have a good time.

When we moved to the Caribbean, where most houses have

a pool, Kesler was only two and didn't know how to swim. The thought of having a pool in our backyard made me very nervous. I'd heard all those terrible stories of children wandering into their pools and drowning. It got so bad that I started having nightmares. So Aaron and I decided that as soon as we got to our new home, we'd teach Kesler how to swim.

Obviously, we wanted Kesler to learn how to swim so he wouldn't drown, but we also didn't want to turn into helicopter parents every time there was water nearby.

After we had moved, we were in the pool with Kesler every day. We started by putting floaties on him, and at the end of every session, we'd take them off for a few minutes and let him put his face in the water. Within a couple of months, Kesler was swimming well enough that if he fell in, he'd be able to get himself to the edge of the pool or be able to turn himself over so that he could call for help.

If you're a family that spends a lot of time near water or in a boat, look into baby floating classes. They teach infants as young as six months old to kick their legs and turn over in the water so they can breathe and float until they're rescued. I didn't believe it myself until I googled it. It's truly amazing and worth checking out.

Everyone thought it was great that Kesler learned to swim so quickly, which was true. We wanted to protect him by giving him the skills to swim on his own, but we were also doing it for ourselves so that we didn't have to watch over him whenever we were in the pool.

Now that Kesler is five, he's a superstrong swimmer. When we go to the rock pool near our current house, I sit on the side with my book, having confidence in his skills and not feeling the need to hover.

DAD BOX

◇◇◇◇◇◇◇◇◇

My Paper Route

I grew up on the west coast of Canada where it's dark and rainy from October to April. My parents were entrepreneurs who owned a grocery store and other businesses. My dad believed that if there was something you wanted to do, you went out and did it.

When I was twelve, I decided I wanted a paper route. I started out with one that was near my house, which was easy. It took me about twenty minutes.

Then I got offered a route that paid more money and was in a neighborhood about five miles from home. The only thing my parents said to me about taking on the new route was that if I started it, I'd have to finish it, no matter what. They weren't going to deliver any papers for me. They gave me a bike and told me to knock myself out. I was off and running!

Every day at 3:30 p.m. when I got out of school, I grabbed my bike and rode off. There was a huge forest behind my school with a deep, dark forest gully that I had to go down and back up in order to get to the main road. From there, it was another two miles to the neighborhood where I delivered papers.

On the way back home, I'd either go through the gully or have to ride an extra mile up north to go around the forest. But that seemed like a waste of time to me and unnecessary work.

When winter arrived, it got dark around 4:30 p.m. Most days, I could make it through the forest before dark on my way to the neighborhood, but on the way back, it was pitch black. I couldn't see my hand in front of my face. Usually, it was raining, windy, cold, and miserable, and there was never anyone around. The forest was one of those perfect places to kidnap and rape someone. In fact, not many years before, there had been a serial killer named Clifford Olson who'd kidnapped kids in the area. It was still pretty fresh in everyone's mind.

There wasn't one night that I wasn't in pure panic going down into the gully. Every time, I'd stop at the top of the hill and question whether to keep going. Some days, I'd ride the extra mile to go around the forest because I was too freaked out. Nine times out of ten, though, I just went down the hill with no brakes so I could hit the bottom with as much speed as possible. On the way back up I pumped my legs until it felt like my lungs were going to burst. I never, ever wanted to come to a full stop in that forest. If I did, I figured I was a sitting duck, and I wasn't going to get duct taped for sure. Every time I made it through, I was just stoked to be alive.

I had that paper route for two years. It taught me discipline and gave me a sense of confidence, a feeling of independence, and the first taste of my own money. Sure, the weather sucked shit, but I showed up almost every day.

By the time I was fourteen, I was so fired up about making money that I went to work for Chuck E. Cheese. After that I got hired at McDonald's. My confidence had grown so much that by the time I was fifteen, I was waiting tables at a restaurant. I was the only kid in high school who could buy my buddies cheese burgers at lunch if I felt like it.

Your kids learn through struggle. They value what they work for. Make them work!

CHAPTER 4

Confidence = Good; Diva = Bad

First and foremost, your kid should have a good sense of self-worth. Here's how to instill it.

I'm a huge fan of *Sex and the City* and still watch reruns. The reason I love it, besides the humor, fashion, sex, and everything New York, is because it's honest, awkward, and real. And at the risk of my husband having to hand over his man card, he started watching it, too. I think part of its likability is that we can all see ourselves in the characters at different stages in our life and can laugh at ourselves for being fucking ridiculous at the best and worst of times.

There was one episode in which the four friends went to the suburbs for a baby shower. None of them, of course, had babies of their own. They were the city girls going to a Stepford wives baby shower. One mother with an infant son in her arms walked up to them and said, "I tell my baby Harry every day that he's a gift from God."

The four friends shared a knowing look, and one of them replied, "Ugh! I pity the woman who marries Harry!"

We all want to praise our kids, encourage them, and give them confidence, but at what point do we start creating an asshole? There's a fine line between instilling self-worth and inflating an ego. When do kids begin to believe that they truly are God's gift? And then how do we carefully knock them off their pedestals once they put themselves up there?

I love this example with Soleil. Soleil is a smart girl and an A student. She's always attended private schools, but after we left the Caribbean, she went to a public school for the first time. Her school in the Caribbean had been a topnotch, highly academic international school.

Math was never Soleil's strongest subject. It's not because she didn't understand the concepts. She never enjoyed math and, as a result, didn't put much effort into it, which her average grade definitely reflected.

Before going to her new school, my husband and I had a talk with Soleil. We pointed out to her that she might be further ahead in certain subjects due to the different curriculums. Her response was, "Oh, I know. I'm sure I'll seem like a genius compared to the other kids." My husband and I looked at each other dumbfounded. What did she just say?

It was a double-edged sword. We were glad Soleil had confidence in her academic skills and felt that she'd be ahead in her class, but at the same time, we didn't want her to continue thinking that way. In truth, when those words came out of her mouth, I thought to myself, *What a little asshole.* My second thought was, *Fuck, what if her new friends think she's an asshole?* There's a balance between being confident and having an exaggerated sense of self-worth. We wanted to bring her back down to earth. It was a perfect teachable moment.

We explained to Soleil that she was probably right and would find that she was ahead of the other kids in some subjects because she'd been able to attend a more academic school, but that certainly wasn't grounds to assume she was a genius.

She'd be quickly disappointed, we told her, if there were kids at the same level or even higher than her in math. Also, she should have some humility entering a new school. If she goes to a new school thinking she's smarter than everyone else, we explained to her, she'd be quickly disliked. "You can't believe you're better than everyone just because you were fortunate enough to go to an academic school," we said. "Yes, you've got good grades, but there are smart kids everywhere. Don't go in thinking you're the best. Go in with humility and earn your place."

Soleil quickly got it. Certainly, the thought of her new friends thinking she was some kind of freak or even a bitch concerned her, given that starting a new school is never easy. Even though she was smart, she may not be the smartest. I want Soleil to be proud she's a straight A student, but I also want her to keep her ego in check. I'm sure we all know some really smart people who are huge assholes.

NO NEED TO COMPARE

It's not just kids who like to compare themselves to others. We adults do it as well. We're quick to compare jobs, incomes, homes, cars, clothes, and general lifestyle. And on top of that, add our competitive edge—who has more, does more, spends more?; who is better at golf, is fitter, or looks like they have more of their shit together? We can be competitive, too. But for our kids' sake, as well as our own, we should focus on personal growth and not on how we're doing compared to another person. We all want validation that we're doing well and succeeding, but isn't it fucked up to look outside ourselves and our partners to get it?

All kids need to understand that even though they're good at something, there'll always be someone who's better. That should be a source of inspiration to work harder and achieve more rather than deflate them.

As an example, my husband and I love to go to Las Vegas—and not just for the obvious reasons like gambling, drinking, shows, and dining. We love to go because we're inspired by the possibilities. I wander through the hotels and shopping malls filled with expensive designer stores, jewels, and extravagant suites. I don't think to myself, *This is bullshit because I'll never afford these things.* I think, *Fuck yeah! I can have all this. It's just going to take more work.* I'm inspired when we're there to become more successful. We could feel defeated by not being able to afford all the opulence, but instead, we're inspired to do better and try harder in our company.

I want my kids to have the same kind of attitude when they encounter someone who's better than them. One of my daughter's best friend, Abbey, was also an A student, except that she was phenomenal at math. While Soleil struggled, she was a natural. Abbey got all As including math and Soleil got all As except math.

Over time, I noticed that Soleil was becoming more competitive with Abbey. One day, I asked Soleil why Abbey had better grades in math because their other grades were the same, and they both had a similar set of study skills. Soleil answered by saying that Abbey spent a lot more time working on math than she did. Bingo! That was exactly why Abbey was achieving better grades than Soleil. I explained to her that there was no reason to feel jealous. If she wanted a perfect report card like Abbey's, then all she had to do was spend more time working on her math.

Seeing someone who's doing better than we are should force us to ask the tough questions about our own efforts. If you feel jealous about someone's success, don't complain. Get off your ass and figure out how you can mimic what they're doing so you aren't the one with regrets. You can apply this to your parenting, too. When you see someone with great kids, ask them questions, watch how they talk to their kids, and learn what you can do to make adjustments to your own skills. Remember, as I've said in previous chapters, your parenting skills will evolve as your kids grow. And that's a good thing.

SELF-RESPECT: YOU GOTTA HAVE IT TO TEACH IT

Teaching your children self-respect and self-worth comes from having it yourself. If you don't value yourself, you can't possibly teach your kids to do it.

Self-worth can be an especially difficult area for women. We tend to be too critical of ourselves. We don't like our body image, or we compare ourselves to other mothers. We can become overly judgmental and not respect ourselves. And then our kids will feel it and see it in us.

One of my pet peeves is mothers who drop their kids off at school in their pajamas. I get why they do. Mornings at our house are a fucking zoo between fixing breakfast and lunches for three; getting everyone dressed, hair combed, and teeth brushed; finding homework from the night before; and gathering bags, boots, and coats! But it also takes only two minutes to pull on a pair of yoga pants and run a brush through your hair or throw on a cap. I am not saying you need to be done up like you're going to a ball, but do have some self-respect. Your snowman jammies are cute at home, but I don't want to see them on the playground. It's even worse when you're still wearing them at 3:00 p.m. when you're picking up your kids after school. Really?!

I work at home and could spend all day in my pajamas if I wanted, but I prefer to present the best version of myself whether I'm at home or not. And I expect my kids to do the same.

I put in the effort to look my best, not just because it makes me feel good, but because I like to have sex with my husband. You may think, *What the fuck is she talking about?* Bear with me. This may sound antifeminist, but if your husband gets tired of you because you never take the time to look nice, he'll start to look elsewhere. I see it time and time again. Husbands (and wives, too, for that matter) want you to look nice for them. There's a reason they were attracted to you in the first place. Just because you have kids with your husband doesn't mean he's tied to you for life. You always have to go the extra mile to keep his interest, in my opinion, and the same goes for him. I want my husband to think I'm sexy and be attracted to me. I want him to want to have sex with me, and I expect the same from him.

Like anything else, self-worth is a learned behavior. If your kids don't see you valuing yourself, they won't learn it. Self-worth and self-respect have a lot to do with other basic things, like how we keep our home. The mother of one of my best friend is a hoarder, and now my friend is seeing the same tendencies in herself. She's starting to get buried under clutter and hates it, but that's what she learned from her mother. I don't want to preach that your home needs to be perfect every moment of the day. There are many days when my breakfast dishes don't get done until after dinner, but they do get done. Take some pride in yourself and your surroundings.

If you want your kids to keep their rooms clean, then you have to model the behavior and show them how it's done.

You can't just tell them to clean their rooms and expect it to happen. They'll mimic what they see you do.

My mom's favorite saying is, "Bleach is your best friend." When I moved into my first apartment, one of the first things she bought me was a bottle of bleach. She's a neat freak. I grew up in a house in which nothing was ever out of place, which was way too extreme for me. Even though I prefer my house to be more casual, I still want it to be clean, and I don't let my kids slide if their rooms are a mess. They think I'm nagging, but I want to establish the behavior so that when they move into their own homes, they'll take pride in their surroundings and in themselves. Healthy self-worth has to be taught.

INVEST IN THE PASSION

It will take time to find out what your kids are passionate about. We all have an image in our head of what we'd like our children to accomplish. I know Soleil loves to dance, so I imagined her as a beautiful ballerina in a tutu and pointe shoes. In reality, she hates ballet and is an amazing hip-hop dancer. Now my image of her includes some wicked hip-hop shoes and a sick beat. Awesome, right?

Even if it shatters the image you have of your child, letting your kids pursue their passions instills self-worth. My son

Everest certainly didn't live up to what his father had in mind for him.

Soccer's been a big part of my husband's life since he was seven years old. Aaron played on both school and league teams and eventually for Canada's national team. So he was pretty stoked when Everest showed interest in the sport. He loved the idea of his first son following in his footsteps.

Everest is not a big kid, so we thought soccer would be a good fit. We signed him up for Timbits Soccer, which offers a great program for young kids. It's casual, gives a good introduction to the sport, and isn't overly competitive.

Everest was almost five at the time. When the season started in September, the weather was still nice, cool but sunny. Aaron was the coach, and Everest enjoyed being out on the field with him. Seeing them together made my heart explode. Everything seemed to be going well. Then the weather started to turn, and practices and games were held in the rain. Everest started to have meltdowns because he was cold. He'd stand at one end of the field while his team was at the other end. It became clear that he wasn't enjoying anything about playing soccer. No matter how much we encouraged him, he just wasn't into it.

We have a rule in our house that whenever our kids make a

commitment to do something, they have to follow through until the end. If they sign up for a league and don't like it partway through the season, they can't quit in the middle because it's not fair to the rest of the team. They can't stop simply because they don't like something. So we told Everest that he had to finish the season, which continued until April, but that he didn't have to play soccer the following year if he didn't want to.

Everest finished the year even though he wasn't thrilled about it. When it was time to sign up for the next season, he told us he didn't like soccer and didn't want to continue. Aaron, of course, was disappointed, but we certainly weren't going to force Everest to play if he didn't want to.

Because Aaron and I are fitness people, sports are a must for our kids. It was obvious to us that Everest didn't like team sports and preferred individual sports, like jiu-jitsu. He's not a competitive kid, but finding out what it was that he was really passionate about took some trial and error. In the end, it turned out not to be a sport at all. He's a gamer and passionate about creating video games and learning how to code.

Instead of trying to hammer a square peg into a round hole and trying to turn Everest into a soccer player, we told him that we'd support whatever it was that he loved. As long as there was continual growth, we would encourage and support him in his love of gaming. He felt respected and worthy of learning. Gaming may even turn into a career for Everest instead of just a hobby. It's always a win-win situation whenever someone can make a living doing what they love. Everest's love of gaming, however, didn't replace our commitment to finding a sport that he could love. It took us time to find his second passion.

Unfortunately, not all parents give their children options because they have something else in mind for them. You can see that in Texas where many boys don't seem to have a choice about playing football. Being able to do what they love is good for a child's soul. Kids who are forced to be someone they aren't feel suffocated, just like people who go to a job that they hate every day.

Give your kids as many opportunities as you can to discover what it is they're passionate about. It's the best way to get them excited about learning, growing, and striving. If they hate what they're doing, watch what assholes they'll become. They'll push back and resent you for making them do what they don't like.

NO DUMBING DOWN

To fit in socially, kids sometimes feel they have to dumb down. We catch our daughter doing it, and I call her out on it all the time. She's a thinker. She likes to analyze a situation carefully, consider things from all angles, and then speak her mind. I'm often surprised at how deep our conversations can be considering she is still young. It makes me so proud to see the woman she is becoming. However, we've noticed, especially when she's with a group of friends, that she has a tendency to say really dumb shit, stuff that I know she knows. And she does it intentionally. Maybe she thinks it makes her sound cool or perhaps she doesn't want to come across as knowing the answer, but for whatever reason, she dumbs herself down.

The phenomenon of dumbing down, according to recent studies, is usually gender specific. Boys, it seems, can be quick to talk about everything they know and how smart they are, whereas girls are more likely to hold back and withdraw because they don't want to come across as if they know it all. When Soleil does this, we don't let her get away with it.

It's important to call your kid out on the spot, whether a girl or a boy, when they're dumbing down. Otherwise, you'll reinforce the behavior. Let your child know it makes a difference how he or she sounds. There's no need for Soleil to make herself come across as less smart than she really is in order to fit in. I want her, and all my kids, to be confident, speak up, and have an opinion. I want Soleil to be perceived as the intelligent, well-rounded girl she is. I don't want her devaluing herself because she thinks it sounds cool.

WALK THE TALK

In our house, we walk the talk.

The best way for kids to prove their skills and intelligence to others is through action. If someone says they're the best in math, then they'd better be getting As. If a kid says he's the best soccer player on the team, then he has to have the skills to back it up. If not, there are two options: either he has to stop being overly confident and exaggerating, or he has to work on his skills until he becomes the best.

In our family, Everest's nickname is "The Mayor." He's an old soul, and some of the things that came out of his mouth when he was only two or three years old shocked us because they were so profound for his age. He started talking in full sentences at fourteen months. It would freak out our friends. They'd walk into a room and be shocked when this little guy who could barely walk was speaking in sentences. He's always been insightful, hilarious, and unique.

I remember one school assembly in particular. It was an awards ceremony and parents were invited. Each class came into the gym one at a time, and on this day, Everest's class was the last to enter. He was about five at the time. As Everest was heading to his seat, all the other kids from preschool through grade eight called out to him and greeted him. He waved to everyone and gave them the thumbs-up, like he was running for the fucking presidency. I thought he looked like a little game show host.

My husband and I were dying of laughter at how cool and calm he was. Everest had charisma and a gift for conversation. For me, the moment was huge. As funny as it was to see him act like that, I realized it wasn't an act. This confident, sociable, and lovable kid was mine. And I had helped mold his personality by supporting who he was. Everest always says, "I'm just doing me, Mom." He already knew at an early age who he is, and more importantly, he's absolutely comfortable with it. Some adults still haven't figured this out. I left that assembly patting myself on the back and saying to myself, *Maybe I do know what I am doing.*

CELEBRATE THE VICTORIES

Celebrate the victories, no matter how small they may be. We do a lot of celebrating in our house, even for small things. It helps build confidence, especially in younger children, and reinforces positive behavior. I'm not saying we throw a party every time someone manages to pee in the toilet and not on the floor, but we do notice and appreciate their effort.

When Kesler was little and getting the hang of taking his plate to the kitchen counter at the end of a meal, I thanked him and told him what a big boy he was. He'd stick out his chest and say, "I am a big boy, Mom." He was so proud of himself. It wasn't a huge moment in his life, but it reinforced positive behavior when it happened. Each time he brought his plate to the counter, he was praised, and eventually, he began to praise himself. He'd announce that he was a big boy so he could get the recognition he was looking for. After a while, he took his plate to the counter, placed it down, and excused himself from the table. Booyah! Habit created!

Soleil's at that age when keeping her room clean is a challenge. I used to do the same thing as a teenager—bowls with spoons stuck to them, wrappers and papers everywhere, clothes and makeup on the floor, the works. But when she does clean her room, whether I've asked her or not, I thank her and let her know I appreciated that she cleaned her room. I don't say, "Thank God, you finally cleaned your room because it was a total mess." Instead of highlighting the negative, you can turn a situation into a celebration by simply changing how you say something.

Before I had kids, I used to watch *Supernanny* when she was first on television. When I look back, I don't know why I watched the show. I didn't have kids and wasn't interested in having any. I think it was because I liked to judge the parents, like we all did before we had kids. I'd think, *Look at those idiots. They've let their fucking two-year-old run their home.* Now I could kick myself for thinking that. I get it now!

Supernanny said something that's always stuck with me: kids are faced with criticism every day. Instead of focusing on things that aren't going well, she encouraged parents to pay attention to the things their kids were doing well. Then, over time, she suggested, you can work on those things your kids aren't good at.

Instead of constantly harping on Soleil about her math grades, for instance, we celebrated the good grades she did get, which didn't take anything away from the fact that she still had to work more on her math. She knew math was her weak spot, so we didn't have to keep hammering on about it. That's parenting from the positive, and we don't do enough of it.

New at the Skate Park

Not long before we moved, we were at a skate park in the Caribbean. One of Everest's friends had invited him to come along even though Everest knew nothing about skateboarding or riding scooters. But he told me he wanted to give it a try, so I bought him a scooter. I used to ride when I was a kid and knew it's not easy to learn and can be scary.

Everest is short and small and has always been the smallest kid in his class.

We headed out to the skate park. His buddies were there, and they were supergood on their scooters. Everest started out slowly and learned to balance and ride the hills. He caught on fairly quickly while the other boys raced past him.

Scooters are either two wheeled or three wheeled. The three-wheelers are for beginners, and the more advanced riders use two-wheelers. Soon, Everest was bombing around and feeling good about himself on his three-wheeled scooter. The kids, as kids do, came by on their two-wheelers and said things to him like, "Look at the baby on the three-wheeled scooter." Everest just turned to them and said, "Hey, guys, don't be ridiculous. You all started out on three-wheeled scooters, too." He instantly deflected their insults without defending himself. He was simply stating a matter of fact.

The boys tried to get under his skin, and he would have none of it. He didn't allow their taunts to bother him. I was so proud of Everest. He had already realized that what other people thought about him didn't matter.

We teach our kids that happiness can never be determined by what anyone else has to say or think about them. If they start letting that happen, they'll go down a deep, dark hole. Each of us is responsible for our own happiness. Everest understood that at a young age. He didn't shrink from the challenge of trying something new and was willing to risk having people make fun of him. He just brushed it off because he knew his self-worth.

CHAPTER 5

You Got to Teach Your Kid to Own Their Own Shit

Teaching your kid to say, "I'm sorry," is great. Teaching your kid how to say sorry and mean it is fucking awesome!

Everest and Soleil were in the swimming pool playing a game of passing the ball back and forth so that it skipped across the water a certain number of times before the other person caught it. Each time they passed the ball back, they had to add another skip. It was tricky, challenging, and fun, and they were having a good time.

Suddenly, Everest threw the ball at Soleil when she wasn't ready and it hit her in the face. It was a big rubber ball, so it wasn't painful, but she got mad instantly. He'd thrown the ball even though she'd told him that she wasn't ready. It caught her off guard, and she was teary. He saw the opportunity to win and acted like an asshole. Everest knew without a doubt that he'd hit Soleil in the face.

I happened to be sitting nearby and made them get out of the pool. We have a rule in our house that when there's an argument or a disagreement, there has to be an apology by one or both people involved. The apology has to be sincere and end with hugging. I know that sounds cheesy, but it makes everyone feel better, especially when they're young.

Everest was obviously in the wrong, although he thought his actions were hilarious. In fact, he had such a shit-eating grin on his face that I had a hard time holding back my own laughter. I told him that he owed Soleil an apology.

He turned to Soleil and said, "I'm sorry that you weren't fast enough to catch the ball."

Bam!

Then she replied, "Well, I'm sorry you weren't smart enough to hear me."

Boom!

It was downhill from there. Before I knew it, the shit talk became worse. My head turned from side to side like I was watching a tennis match. They took turns lobbing insults at each other. I appreciate a good burn as much as the next person, but this was the complete opposite of what an apology should be.

Teaching your children to apologize and say I'm sorry is a learned behavior. Kids always have an excuse for why something happened. "I didn't do it on purpose" or "It was just an accident" are popular ones. You have to teach your kids to say, "I'm sorry," and mean it. If you don't, they'll never be able to do it as adults. I have friends who literally can't say the words *I'm sorry*, which makes them look like a complete asshole.

It's even more difficult to meet in the middle when both of you are wrong. People prefer to shift the blame so that one person is right and the other one is wrong. We teach our kids that they can both be right and wrong, that it's OK to agree to disagree and call it a day.

NOT ALL APOLOGIES ARE EQUAL

At our house, we have rules for what an acceptable apology is:

1. First and foremost, the apology has to be sincere; no sarcasm allowed.

2. The apology has to be immediate.

3. Both participants have to make eye contact.

This can be even harder for adults to do. Being engaged and present in a conversation or in an apology means looking a person directly in the eye. Shifty eyes equal a bullshit apology in my experience.

4. There's nothing to be embarrassed about if you're wrong and you say you're sorry.

Hopefully, you get better at saying you're sorry as you get older because there's no shame in it. And believe me, there are times when I'd rather stab myself in the eye than admit I'm sorry. If Aaron and I are having a debate about something in front of the kids and I'm wrong—as hard as it is to believe that could be true—I say to him that I'm sorry I didn't understand what he'd been trying to say or that I didn't have all the information. I want my kids to see how a disagreement ends in a healthy way.

5. The apology ends with a hug.

We started the hugging as soon as our kids were old enough to talk. If they did something wrong, we'd ask them what they had to say about it and then always had them end with a hug. We don't want anyone to harbor unexpressed feelings in our house. If someone does anything wrong, we deal with it and move on. There's nothing more unhealthy and detrimental to a relationship than holding on to a grudge. It's simply not worth the negative energy.

TEACH ACCOUNTABILITY

When I first encountered *Minecraft*, I thought it was some old video game from the 1980s because of the graphics. I didn't realize it was a new game. Soleil was the first in our house to start playing it. She loved the creativity of building houses, castles, and other elements of the game. Then Everest started playing when he got old enough. He liked the creepers and fighting zombies, and ultimately, he taught Kesler to play, who loved it, too.

Kesler loved talking about killing zombies with Everest. They'd play on the same server so they could be in the same world and attack zombies together. After a while, Kesler became obsessed with the game. As soon as he got home from school, he'd start hunting zombies, and then he'd go to school the next day and talk about it with his teachers and classmates. His teachers knew *Minecraft* and understood the context for what Kessler was saying, but most of the kids in his class didn't. Often, they were a first child in the family and had no older siblings to introduce them to the game at an early age like Kesler did.

Eventually, Kesler's teacher contacted us and said that Kesler was scaring his classmates with all his talk of shooting zombies and asked that Kesler no longer share his stories at school. Part of me was like, *Are you fucking serious? It's just a game! Kesler wasn't showing the kids anything; it was just words.* But, of course, I also understood that killing zombies was not what the average four-year-old is comfortable talking about.

It was tough on Kesler because he was so enthusiastic about *Minecraft*, but our job was to teach him how to be accountable when he was at school.

We sat down with Kesler and explained that talking about killing zombies to his friends who knew nothing about *Minecraft* was scaring them. We'd talk about zombies only at home. He totally understood and agreed, but the next day, he went back to school and talked about zombies again. Another phone call from his teacher, another apology from me, and another moment of feeling like a failure as a mother. Then a quick glass of wine and I was back at it!

Each morning on the drive to school, we kept reminding Kesler so that he wouldn't forget. He always agreed, but it took several days before he was finally able to stop. We kept him accountable until it became a habit. He was still fully engaged in the game and talked about killing zombies at home but no longer at school. It came down to a simple reminder that there was to be no zombie talk at school. There were no consequences, only a friendly reminder.

Too often, parents want to jump in and defend their children's actions because they don't want their kids to be wrong or get in trouble. But failure equals growth. We fail, we learn, and then we grow, over and over again. It's far better to teach your kid that it's OK to be wrong, make a mistake, and be accountable. Sometimes kids don't even know when they've done something wrong, like Everest when he borrowed a book.

At Everest's school in the Caribbean, each teacher kept a small personal library in the classroom to supplement the large school library. Students in the class could sign a book out for a week and take it home.

One day, Everest's teacher asked him to deliver a note to another teacher. The other teacher wasn't in her classroom when he arrived, so he left the note on her desk. While he was there, he took a look at the books she had in her library collection and saw one on *Minecraft*. He was excited to find it and brought it back with him to his classroom to read at quiet time.

That evening, Everest brought the book home, and I asked him where he'd gotten it. When he said from Miss Susan's classroom, I asked if she'd allowed him to take the book out of her room. He stopped and realized that he hadn't asked because she hadn't been there at the time. He told me he had taken the book back to his own classroom to read.

There was no ill intention on Everest's part when he took the book, which was part of the classroom library collection like the one in his classroom where the rule was you could borrow a book and return it a week later.

Obviously, because it hadn't been his own classroom, Everest should have asked Miss Susan's permission before he took the book. He got upset because he didn't want anyone thinking he had stolen the book.

The next day, we took him to Miss Susan's classroom and had him explain to her that he'd taken the book but that he hadn't intended to steal it. He did it because he was so excited to read about *Minecraft*.

Of course Miss Susan wasn't upset. However, we still made

him say he was sorry even though it was an innocent mistake. He wasn't embarrassed because he understood that he had not followed the rules and was taking responsibility. It may seem like we were being hard assed, but it was another teachable moment with a powerful lesson that could have been easily overlooked.

RETALIATION AND WHAT TO DO ABOUT IT

It's a kid's nature to want to retaliate, especially when they're young and feel they've been wronged or were physically hurt.

In Kesler's first year of school, he went to prekindergarten for a half day. A little boy, whom we ended up calling "the biter," was in his class. Nearly every day for an entire year he bit Kesler. Often, it was a little bite, but a few times, he bit hard enough to break the skin and bleed.

Kesler and this kid, who was only two, had a love-hate relationship. They loved to play with each other, but when the little boy got frustrated and didn't know how to express himself, he bit Kesler.

This went on for the entire year. With the first few bites, I did my best to be understanding. I knew when kids are learning to coexist for the first time in a school environment, it doesn't always go smoothly. However, after six or seven bites, I became fucking livid! I wanted to say, "How hard is it to teach your kid not to make my kid fucking bleed?" I also knew that the kid's mom was very upset that this behavior was defining her son. I tried to stay calm as I knew the mom was working on helping her son not to bite, but every day, it was extremely frustrating and a big challenge for me to keep from losing my mind. Kesler was getting bit because the two of them liked to play together. It was a catch-22 situation: the kids wanted to be together, but when the little boy got angry, he retaliated out of frustration and bit Kesler.

The next year, the same little boy was in Kesler's class. I crossed my fingers, hoping that now that the boy was a year older, he'd learned not to bite and there'd be no more issues.

About a week into school, the biter struck again, and Kesler snapped! Kesler probably didn't want to go through another year of being bit. He turned around and punched the boy, and the two of them started wrestling. They punched and kicked each other and both got a time-out from their teacher for fighting on the playground.

When the school called to inform me of what happened, I was instantly proud that Kesler got a shot off and stood up for himself. I felt he'd redeemed himself after a year of being tortured by the kid. The parent side of me, on the other hand, knew I wouldn't be teaching Kesler anything valuable by telling him how proud I was that he had leveled his friend on the playground. I didn't want to celebrate the fact that he beat up this little boy even though in my head I thought he deserved it. More importantly, I wanted to teach Kesler to be accountable for his actions.

When I spoke to Kesler about what had happened, I told him that I understood why he hit the biter, that he'd been mad and frustrated. I also said that hitting your friends is wrong.

We took Kesler to meet with his school friend and made him apologize for punching him, despite the fact that we knew he wasn't entirely in the wrong. It was never OK, though, to retaliate by hitting a friend: two wrongs don't make a right. I'm sure it wasn't easy for Kesler to say he was sorry after all those bites, but he learned the bigger lesson about accountability when he did.

We have wrestling time in our house, which helps in situations like this. Some boys naturally like to fight. We want our boys to wrestle, tussle around with each other, and have a good time, including with their dad. One of the boys will yell, "Wrestle time," and all three of them run to join in, usually on our bed where they can pillow fight and wrestle safely. We also establish boundaries to encourage the right behavior at the right time. We make it very clear that fighting never takes place with friends on a field or at school where someone can get hurt and only takes place at home, because who wouldn't want to be a WWE wrestler from time to time?

SOME THINGS NEVER NEED AN APOLOGY

There are things that kids should absolutely never have to apologize for. Your kid should never be sorry for anything he or she earned through hard work—for getting good grades, for being the top in the class, or for earning awards, recognition, and trophies. Kids should be proud of their accomplishments.

My daughter, Soleil, likes to write fantasy stories. She posts them online a chapter at a time, each story ending with a cliffhanger. A little community has formed around her stories. She now has more than a thousand people following her posts, which she finds superexciting, and I think is awesome. She loves being an online blogger and posting stories and videos, and enjoys her mini-celebrity status. A friend of Soleil also posts stories but has only a couple hundred followers. When her friend said how lucky Soleil was to have a thousand people reading her stories, Soleil told her friend she was sorry. She apologized because she felt bad that her friend wasn't doing as well as she was.

I like it that Soleil is sensitive to her friend's feelings and not gloating, but at the same time, I don't want Soleil feeling sorry for being successful. She should be proud that people enjoy her writing and sense of humor and should never apologize for doing well. I want her to celebrate her success while not feeling the need to brag or think she's the best. There's a fine line between the two, but there's never any need to apologize for well-earned greatness.

◇◇◇◇◇◇◇◇◇◇

Soleil's iTunes

When your kids shit the bed—and they will—you've got to make them own it. It's superuncomfortable to do, so most parents shy away from it. Nobody wants to have those difficult conversations. The problem with not holding your kids accountable is that the behavior becomes habitual, and kids don't learn that there are consequences for their actions.

When we had our first iPad, we had an iTunes account that we kept open so that we didn't have to always log on.

One day, a credit card bill arrived with a charge of $872. I looked at it and thought, *What the fuck?* First, I asked Liz if she'd gone on a buying rampage, and she hadn't. Then I opened up the iTunes account and checked the history. It was loaded with charges for extra stuff from games, like gems, jewels, and money bags.

I put two and two together and realized that Soleil was buying in-app purchases for the games she was playing. My instant response was that the purchases hadn't been clearly identified and that my daughter had been taken advantage of. So I checked out the games and looked at the things she'd bought, which were premium dresses and jewels for her dolls or advancement to a higher level of the game. I also checked out how easy or hard it was to make a purchase. Sure enough, a window popped up for each purchase stating the amount of money the item cost and prompting the buyer to respond with a yes or no to continue. It was clear that Soleil knew what she'd been doing and was spending real money.

Next thing I did was call iTunes. I explained that my kid had screwed up and asked if there was anything they could do. They said that for one time only, they'd drop the charge to $200.

Then I went to Soleil, who was about eight at the time, old enough to read but still young. I sat her down and told her that I'd just received the iTunes bill. She looked at me blankly, and then I said it was $872. I explained that all the charges were for purchases in five games, which I listed for her. Her face went white. And I had to try hard to stay strong—her little face was so sad and I adored her so.

I asked her if she'd bought items in those games. Instantly, she teared up and answered yes.

"Did you know that you were spending real money on those things?"

I could tell she was processing in her head the answer that she wanted to give me: *Am I going to lie? Am I going to tell the truth?*

I went on, "You knew that you were spending real money, didn't you?" She burst into tears and said yes. And then I asked her why she did it, and she answered that she didn't know.

I told her that in this world, when you spend money, there are consequences. I didn't want all the stuff she'd bought, so I wasn't going to pay for it. She'd have to pay for it.

I also explained that I'd called Apple, and they, fortunately for her, had reduced the bill from $872 to $200, and that she wasn't worth more than $5 an hour doing work for me. So she owed me $200 divided by $5, or forty hours of work to pay off the bill.

She was OK with that. We put a chart up, and I had

her do menial tasks around the house and in the yard for forty hours over the next two months.

Of course, I could've just paid the $200, but here was an important opportunity to hold her accountable for her choices. It wasn't a mistake. She'd made a choice, and she paid for it.

CHAPTER 6

There's a Difference between Giving and Earning

———

Giving gifts is fun sometimes. But teaching your kid how to start providing for him-/herself is even better.

When I was growing up, money was a taboo subject. Although I still think it's a good idea to teach your kids not to ask an adult how much money he or she makes out of respect, talking about money shouldn't be off-limits.

When Everest and Soleil were little, there were days when I needed to get out of the house. We all have days when the walls are closing in, and we just need to be a part of the outside world. So on a rainy day after being stuck inside for hours, I'd take the kids to the Walmart down the road and wander the aisles. It would break up the day and give us something to do.

After a while, I started buying them each a little treat—nothing fancy, maybe a book of stickers or a can of Play-Doh that didn't cost much. It was a little something for them, and somewhat selfishly, I knew that when we got home, they'd want to play with whatever it was they got and I'd have a bit more time without having to entertain them or think of things for them to do. It was a win-win for everyone.

What I didn't realize at the time was that I was creating a behavior of expectation every time we went out. I didn't notice it at first until one day when we were getting into the car to go downtown to the big mall and they asked me if we could go to Toys R Us. I said sure. I got everyone strapped in, and while I was driving, I heard the two of them in the back seat having a conversation. They were talking about what they were planning on getting, and their list was long. Somehow, a little treat had gone from something small like a bag of marbles or a mini Matchbox car to a major purchase like a baseball bat or a pair of ice skates. Suddenly, I thought to myself, *What have I done?!* They were so sure they were going to get something. I'd created two greedy little assholes who expected that every time we went shopping, they'd get a toy.

As we wandered the aisles of Toys R Us, they'd point to things and ask to have them, and each time I said, "No, not today." Confused and concerned, they continued to ask until we'd made our way through the last aisle and exited the store. As hard as it was for me, they got nothing that day. They couldn't understand why they weren't getting a treat. They were mad and upset. The worst part about it was that I had only myself to blame. I'd created the monster, the bad habit, but I could also undo it.

From that day forward, there was a complete reversal every time we went shopping. As I strapped the kids into the car, I'd preface our trips by reminding them that we were just looking and that there'd be no special treat. Every time they asked for something, I said no. It was shocking for them. It took a while to break the habit, but it was important to start teaching them about earning a treat instead of automatically assuming they deserved one. By sticking to the strategy, they eventually stopped asking. It was then that small treats started again but only once in a while, which made them truly special treats.

That's why it's important to talk with your kids about money in a positive light.

Many families go through financial struggles, and it's important for kids to be aware of how much things cost and how hard people have to work to be able to purchase things. The way you speak with kids about money requires maintaining a balance between the facts and how much information is appropriate for your kids to know.

We had friends who were struggling with money. He was a contract worker and often out of work for six months at a time. It was feast or famine in his industry. So when he had work, they suddenly lived like Wall Street ballers, but as soon as his contract ended, they had little to live on. Their kids would often come over to our house to play. One afternoon, their six-year-old happened to mention that they'd had pancakes for dinner the night before because they didn't have any money to buy meat. WTF?!

It's one thing to tell your kids that their dad doesn't have a lot of work at the moment so everyone needs to be careful with how they spend money. But it may be going too far when a young child knows dinner is pancakes because there's no money. There's no need to scare your kids. You don't want them going to bed at night fearful they won't eat the next day or that they'll lose their home, even if it is a reality. I understand that this is the case for many families and don't judge it, but I do think our kids have many years ahead of them to worry about bills and finances. If we can protect them from that stress when they're children, it's one less thing for them to worry about.

There's a way to talk about money with your kids that won't scare them. You can teach them to be aware of what things cost, budgeting, and how to be financially smart. As they grow, you can introduce them to paychecks, rent or mortgage payments, and taxes. It can begin with something as simple as opening a bank account for your child or having a jar for saving change. The important thing is that learning starts at home.

Most schools today don't teach kids basic life skills. They don't explain what credit cards are, interest rates, mortgages, or how to balance a checkbook, open a bank account, or fill out a rental application. I think it's tragic. Who gives a fuck about the difference between a rhombus and an isosceles triangle if the average high school teenager doesn't know how to fill out a job application? Perhaps if the education system included basic financial life skills, our country wouldn't be seeing the level of personal debt the average individual is carrying.

When I got out of high school and went to university, I was offered a credit card first thing. The limit was only $500, but I maxed it out pretty quickly. Instant access to $500 meant shopping and treating my friends to dinner with every drink on me. I'd pay off some of it and then start charging again because my limit was manageable, which led, of course, to my credit limit being increased. The more they gave me, the more I spent until it got to the point where the best I could do was pay the interest only. We've all been there. We all know that making the interest payment means shit. It only buys you enough time until you can make a small lump sum payment. And then guess what? You run it up again.

Not long ago when we were about to move into our new house, our kids told us they wanted a hot tub, which sounded pretty good to me. More importantly, it provided us with an opportunity for a teachable moment. We asked our kids how much they thought a hot tub would cost. Everest said we could get one for about $500. Soleil, being more knowledgeable, disagreed and said it would cost around $2,000. Then we discussed the relationship between the cost of the hot tub and the amount of work it would take to pay for it. We also talked about the fact that, compared to school supplies or groceries, a hot tub may not be such a high priority. Having lived in the Caribbean for a few years where incomes are high, the kids were probably not aware of those realities.

Young kids generally don't know what people get paid for the work they do, so it's hard for them to wrap their minds around what things cost. I remember once we were driving down the highway and an amazing red Lamborghini passed us. Everest was impressed. "Did you see that car?" Aaron replied that it was a Lamborghini, a very expensive car. Everest said, "I know, Dad. I bet it costs about $1,000, right?" Yet at the same time he thought a chocolate bar cost $20. As parents, we have to find ways to provide our kids with some perspective.

INSTILL GRATITUDE, NOT ENTITLEMENT

Entitled children are used to getting what they want. Take my daughter's friend. He's a single child from a big-income family, and every year at Christmas, he makes a list of what he wants. His parents use it as a shopping list and buy him everything on it. Last year, he got a computer, an iPad, and an iPhone.

Part of me thinks that's fabulous. If parents are financially successful and that's what they want to do for their children, there's nothing wrong with it. However, they should be careful not to set their child up for a huge let-down later in life. Unless he has the means to sustain the lifestyle and income of his parents after he leaves home, he'll be disappointed, especially if he wasn't taught anything about the realities of money. His parents will have created a little bubble, which in the long run may do him more harm than good.

Money without effort leads to entitlement. Kids need to understand the relationship between hard work, money, and buying things. If you don't teach it to them, they won't learn gratitude as well as how to fend for themselves. Maybe Soleil's friend will put a Ferrari on his Christmas list when he's sixteen and expect to get it, too, but there'll be nothing special about it if he does because he's already gotten everything he wanted for sixteen years. He won't know what it means to be grateful.

Like everything else, gratitude is a learned behavior and is often overlooked by parents because we struggle with feeling grateful ourselves. With busy schedules, financial pressures, and general stress, we often indulge in pity parties instead of being grateful for what we've achieved. I'm definitely guilty of taking a glass of wine to my bathtub at the end of a stressful day and crying. Sound pathetic? It is, but it's how I reset and refocus my gratitude. I let myself feel sorry for myself for the duration of the bath. I get it all out of my system. Then I take a few moments to be grateful for the amazing life I've created. I remind myself I have happy, healthy children, a strong and loving marriage, a bed to sleep in, and food to eat. It's these basic things in life that we need to teach our children to be grateful for.

We don't often sit down together as a family every night of the week at the dinner table, but we do make it a priority to eat together at least three times a week. Recently, when we were having dinner, Kesler wanted everyone to go around the table and share their feelings. It started as, "I feel happy today because I got an A on my test." Now it's become a moment for sharing what we're grateful for during the week. And the best part is there is no wrong answer. I know that by instilling gratitude in my children, they are less likely to be ungrateful assholes when they grow up.

TEACHING THE VALUE OF MONEY

Doing chores and getting an allowance helps kids learn the value of money. How you decide to organize chores in your family may be different than for another family. It's a personal decision.

In our situation, we believe that there are certain things a family does together to maintain the harmony of the home, and we don't feel like we should pay our kids to do them, like cleaning their rooms, putting their dishes in the dishwasher, picking up after themselves, and caring for their animals. In order for us to be able to spend time together as a family, each of us has to pitch in. That's what works in our family.

It took time to establish the system, which was the result of a huge meltdown on my part. It was a Sunday, a miserable dark and rainy day. Aaron was watching football, Soleil had gone to the movies with friends, and the boys were playing in the basement. Everyone was doing exactly what they wanted to be doing, except me. I spent six hours doing laundry, cleaning rooms, washing bathrooms, and making sure everyone was set for the week to come. I was busting my ass for everyone else so they could enjoy their Sunday, and the tantrum that followed was ugly. Why was I the only one doing all the work? Why was I the only one who got zero downtime on the weekend? No wonder come Monday morning I was always fucking exhausted. This is when I realized that things needed to change.

We also have what we call the "above and beyond" chore list. Those are extra chores that the kids can do to earn money. For example, I'll pay them to pick up dog poo in the yard (you can imagine how often that chore gets picked despite the large dollar amount attached to it). If Soleil wants to mow the lawn, she'll get paid for it because it's an extra chore. Essentially, we have two levels of chores: those chores without pay that are expected as a member of the family and those chores that earn money.

If the kids want to work harder, they'll get paid for their time. I want to teach to them that their spare time is valuable, and I want to reward them for being willing to go above and beyond the basic expectations.

Again, what works will differ from family to family. Friends of ours are superorganized and use a daily checklist for their kids. Each kid has a board with a daily list of things to do—making their beds, doing homework, feeding the animals, etc. They check off what they've done, and at the end of each day, one of the parents has to sign off. If everything is signed off by the end of the week, they get their allowance. It's a good system for the right family and teaches kids that if they work hard all week, they'll be rewarded for their effort. It also teaches accountability.

Soleil is also learning that time equals money in another way. We pay her for babysitting, which I feel is appropriate for two reasons: first, we'd be paying someone else to babysit if she wasn't doing it, and second, we're asking her to give up her time to watch the boys even if they're her brothers and the work is easy. She keeps an eye on them, gives them snacks, makes sure they brush their teeth and get their jammies on, and puts them to bed. She's doing a service for us, and I want her to appreciate that her time is valuable.

Hard Work Pays Off

When I was growing up, my dad constantly made me work outside mowing the lawn, pulling weeds, trimming grass, and so on. He simply told me those were my jobs. It wasn't up for negotiation. I hated it, but he knew what he was doing. He was helping me realize that work in this life is required, whether you like it or not.

We do the same thing with our kids. It'd be a whole lot easier if I did things myself, but the benefit is larger when I make my kids do the work. A perfect example is the dog run we built when we lived in the Caribbean.

It was hot, one hundred degrees with 90 percent humidity. I'd laid down some landscaping cloth in the front yard and had about four thousand pounds of loose rock delivered on top of it. The rock had to be shoveled into a wheelbarrow, taken to the backyard, dumped, and spread around.

I took my shirt off, put on my boots, and grabbed the two boys, telling them that we were going outside to do some work. Immediately, they wanted to know what it was they'd have to do, and I told them not to worry about it.

We went outdoors, and I took my shovel, gave them each a little one, and explained that we were taking all the rock to the backyard wheelbarrow by wheelbarrow. Their instant response was that it'd take forever, but I said we'd be working for only a couple of hours. Then they complained that it was too hot, which I wouldn't listen to. "Everyone has to participate in making this house run. Pick up your shovel, and instead of whining, start digging so we can be done."

Then they started scooping, and the miracle that always happens happened. After the first bucket was loaded, they started having fun because, hormonally, whenever we make progress, we get a release of endorphin, which incidentally is why humans evolved so fast compared to other species. We get a hit of dopamine every time we check off the box when we've finished something.

So they filled the first wheelbarrow, and I wheeled it to the backyard and dumped it. Now that they were having fun, they wanted to spread the rock, too. It started with a "no" and went to having fun. Then they got hot. Right away the little one asked if he could go inside and watch TV. My answer was no. I knew there was only a certain amount of heat he could stand before he'd get heat stroke, but he wasn't there yet. Now he was scooping eight rocks or fewer at a time, all the while complaining about how hot it was.

I made him keep going for another fifteen minutes or so, and then I patted him on the bum and sent him inside. Then my other son wanted to stop, too, but he was nine and could handle things a bit longer. He was sweating, and we were shoveling and getting closer to being done. When he started to get pale, I took the shovel from his hand, patted him on the head, and told him that he'd done great work and that I was proud of him. I told him to go inside, too, and drink some water.

I forced both of them to do something they didn't want to do, and I made them feel good about what they were doing while they were doing it. When they were done, I sent them inside, but not before they'd been pushed to the point of being challenged because that's what creates strength. At the end, when I was done, I showed them the dog run that we'd built together. I high-fived them and told them how proud they should be. I wanted them to remember that hard work pays off.

CHAPTER 7

Disciplining Sucks, but You Pay Now or Later

Disciplining is one of the least fun parts of parenting. But there's no avoiding it. Let the punishment fit the crime, and don't let your kid out on parole.

One reason there're so many asshole kids today is, it seems to me, because parents are afraid to punish them. Whether it's because parents don't think it's necessary or don't want to be bothered with following through, they'll often give only a small slap on the wrist as a form of discipline. I hear lots of "Don't do that" or "Please stop that" on the playground only to see a child repeat the same behavior. Kids aren't afraid of consequences because their parents haven't established any history of giving them, on top of which parents just want their children to like them all the time. God forbid we should upset our kids or make them mad at us! But it's our job as parents to correct their behavior. We're not here to be friends with our kids, which is not to say we don't want loving, trusting, and open relationships with them.

When I was sixteen, one night I came home late past curfew, not just a few minutes late but a few hours late. I knew I was in trouble because my dad was waiting for me. I don't think there's anything worse than pulling into your driveway late at night and seeing your dad waiting on the front porch. Shit.

We started to argue. I gave him every excuse why I was late and every reason why my curfew should be extended. I told him that I didn't know why we couldn't just have a conversation like friends. I didn't understand why he had to yell at me.

His response always stuck with me. He turned to me and said, "I don't need any more friends."

At first I was hurt, being an emotional teenager at the time. Later, after I'd calmed down, we had a conversation about it. He explained to me that, as my dad, his job was to give me rules and guidelines, enforce them when I broke them, and help me become a good person. He knew I would make mistakes, but he loved me and would help me rise after I fell. It would, he said, help make me the person I wanted to be—strong, independent, and thoughtful of other people. I had enough friends at school to joke and hang around with, and he had enough friends, too.

I thought about that incident when I had kids of my own. I have a unique relationship with each of my kids, and those relationships are independent of the ones they have with their dad. Although I cherish those moments when there's a connection with my kids, my job is to be their mom first.

A lot of parents live vicariously through their children. I see it even more now that my daughter Soleil is getting older. Moms of teenage girls like to relive the time when they were young and carefree and the world of romance was ahead of them. They want to be part of what their daughters are going through and be one of the girls again.

There's a fine line between relating to your daughter and being her friend. I always want to have a good relationship with my daughter, stay open to any conversation, and be able to get in our jammies together, snuggle under a blanket with a bowl of popcorn, and watch movies.

Soleil got her period recently, which is a big deal when you're twelve. She called right away to tell me and was, not surprisingly, angry and upset. I told her that I got it and felt the same way every month! I loved that she wanted to tell me first and felt comfortable discussing her body and this important milestone with me. It made me think back to when I first got my period. I waited for weeks to tell my mom. We had a different kind of relationship. As much as I loved my mom, our bodies and menstruation were taboo. My mom was comfortable letting the school teach me what I needed to know.

Aaron, on the other hand, had an open relationship with his mom, who raised him as a single mom until he was about six years old. He'd happily ride his bike to the corner store to buy her tampons if she needed them. He knew all there was to know at age six about getting your period. It set the foundation for an open relationship with his mom as he became a teenager. All subjects were open in his house, and it's something we've worked hard to establish in our home.

You have to find the right balance. It's one thing to be the cool mom your daughter's friends are comfortable with, and they want to hang out at your house. It's going too far when moms want to be a part of their daughter's sleepover, take part in the gossip, and insert themselves in their daughter's world. It's important to respect your kids and let them have their own experiences.

ONE PUNISHMENT DOESN'T FIT ALL

There are many ways to discipline children. There isn't one way that fits every family or every child. Children respond to different forms of punishment.

When our youngest son, Kesler, got in trouble, we used to send him to his room for a time-out as punishment. Once when I told him his time was up and he could come out of his room, he said, "Nope, I'm good." I went to his room and discovered that he'd pulled out all his toys and was building a fort. That's when it dawned on me that sending him to his room was not a punishment. All his toys and books were there, so it was a fun place to be.

Even though I found it amusing that he was perfectly happy being in his room for a time-out, it was completely defeating the purpose. Before then, I never understood why he was OK with getting time-outs. I used to think I was an amazing parent because my child went willingly to his room when he was punished. Then I realized that he wanted to be there.

I learned from that experience that the consequence has to suit the crime. It has to resonate with the child so that he or she feels punished. Being sent to your room with your toys and books may not be the answer for every kid. It certainly wasn't for Kesler.

Sometimes your child simply needs a break, and that's important, too. My middle son often says he wants some time alone. At first, I was overprotective and immediately assumed there was something wrong. Was he OK? Was he sick? Were his feelings hurt? Did he have a bad day at school? Then I realized, after driving him insane, that he simply wanted some time to himself. He's OK separating himself from the rest of the family. For Everest, on the other hand, sending him to his room for a time-out is devastating. He doesn't like it when he's intentionally removed from everyone. It's a severe punishment for him, whether his room is full of toys or not.

In order for the punishment to be effective, it has to be child specific. What works for one kid won't necessarily work for the other.

QUICKER IS BETTER

Punishments and consequences don't have to be long-drawn-out affairs to be effective. Now when Kesler messes up, he has to sit in a chair by himself in the corner of the room, do nothing, and talk to no one. It's torture for him, so it doesn't take long for him to change his behavior. For Soleil, it's losing her phone. It's like cutting off one of her limbs because the phone is her lifeline to her friends. When she can't connect with her squad, it's dramatic.

I prefer the short-and-sweet punishment because, in truth, that's all it should take. Being grounded for a week creates a massive inconvenience for the entire family. I don't have the time to monitor a week-long punishment. We're in and out of the house for work, practices, and games. Grounding someone to his or her room for a week wouldn't be an easy sentence in our house because we're always on the move. If we want to inflict longer lasting pain, we have the kids do a chore outdoors, like cleaning up dog shit. Then at least we're getting some cheap physical labor at the same time.

NO WARNING IS BETTER THAN TOO MANY

Parents who are unwilling to discipline their kids or afraid to dole out consequences can easily fall into the habit of giving warnings instead of punishment. After fifteen times of hearing "This is your last warning," kids catch on. They know they can just keep on doing whatever it is they've been doing for a while longer because all they'll get is one more warning.

Warnings don't carry any fear if they're issued too often. There's no urgency for a child to stop the behavior. We have a one-warning policy in our house, and we stick to it every single time. My kids know they get one warning and then there's a consequence. It's nonnegotiable.

The one-warning policy can be tricky to enforce, depending on where you happen to be. If you're at a friend's home or out in public, you still have to stick to the rule. This can be especially hard because, let's be honest, we're all afraid of being judged, and then we're less likely to follow through. You'll need to get over it. If you're out of your house as often as we are, then parenting is going to have to take place everywhere. If you have one set of rules at home and another set of rules for when you're out, your kids will continue to test the boundaries to see how much more they can get away with.

It doesn't matter whether you have a one-warning or a three-warning system, you've got to follow through consistently. Otherwise, warnings won't work. If there's no action backing up your words, things will escalate and get out of hand. Kids will keep pushing, Mom will reach her limit and explode, and everyone will end up mad and crying. If you stick to one or two warnings and follow through with action, you can avoid creating a volatile situation. If you can't follow through, then it's better to say nothing at all.

My sister uses a good system in her classroom that could work equally well at home. It's a three-strikes-and-you're-out system. Whenever a student strikes out, or misbehaves, she puts their name on the board and a red X next to it. That way, all the kids can see where they and everyone else in the class stands and have the chance to take responsibility for their behavior. They'll know when they have to start toning things down. After a while, she found, the kids started to govern themselves. They'd remind one another to quiet down because they could see when someone had two strikes against them. It could seem like she is singling kids out, but she was holding them accountable for their actions. Amazingly, their peers began to hold them accountable, too, which she didn't expect.

A friend of mine uses a variation of the method at her house to reinforce positive behavior. She keeps two jars on the kitchen counter. One is filled with little rubber bouncy balls and the other jar is empty. Every time her child misbehaves, gets punished, or has a time-out, she moves a bouncy ball into the empty jar. From day to day, her child can gauge his behavior. If at the end of the week all the balls have been moved into the "bad" jar, there's work to be done. If the balls stay in the "good" jar, then a special treat is possible. Everyone can monitor what's going on, although the system is geared more to younger kids. If I did this with Soleil, she'd likely sneak downstairs and change the balls in her favor.

A HEALTHY SENSE OF FEAR

Aaron and I both think that a healthy sense of fear is missing these days. I'm often shocked when we're out to see how openly defiant and rude kids can be to their parents, and the parents are OK with it or at least unwilling to deal with the behavior in public. I want to slap them in the head and say, "Wake the fuck up! You're being played, and you're creating a little asshole."

When I was growing up, I was afraid of disappointing my parents more than anything else, especially my dad. I questioned a lot of my decisions more out of fear of upsetting my parents than of receiving a consequence for my behavior. My mom was the master of the silent treatment, and I dreaded her finger.

As kids, my sister and I were dragged along to a lot of social events, and we hated it. My dad was president of the Rotary Club and the chamber of commerce and sat on a lot of boards. This was back in the day when cocktail parties were big. My mom used to spend hours in the kitchen making an amazing spread of food for those weekend parties. Although my sister and I were forced to stay downstairs in our family room when the guests arrived, we still had to have our hair curled and dresses on. Putting a dress on for me was torture!

When we were out, we were bored and looked for ways to entertain ourselves in the sea of adults. If we did something my mom thought was inappropriate, she gave us what we now call the "family finger." She'd catch our eye and take her pinky finger and rub it at the corner of her eye or touch the end of her nose. She always used her pinky finger, and we knew what it meant: we should stop immediately doing whatever it was we were up to. It was the family signal for: stop what you are fucking doing now!

We also knew we'd be in trouble later, which was even worse because we'd have to go through the rest of the evening knowing we'd done something wrong. On the car ride home, we'd hear about it. It wasn't necessarily big trouble, but my mom always used to flash the family finger. Even now, she holds up her pinky when she gets frustrated or we're being sarcastic with her. It's become a running joke in our house.

My mom's finger strategy was very effective. She always followed through, and my dad always backed her up. My parents could have been poster parents for a united front. I never once saw them disagree about a punishment in front of us.

MISBEHAVING IN PUBLIC

Nobody wants to parent in public anymore, which is unfortunate. As parents, we should be understanding when children act out in public and parents need to intervene. Sometimes you have to discipline your children when it's not convenient. Even though spanking is often controversial,

I'm not against it. In our home, it's a last resort. I've spanked my three kids, at most, only five times total. Spanking in public, however, should never be done. It's embarrassing for children to have their pants pulled down. The embarrassment itself will be more damaging to your child than the spanking. But that doesn't mean we shouldn't punish our children in other ways in public.

I know when I've seen someone yell or reprimand a child in public, I've been guilty of blaming and judging the mom. I've caught myself thinking that she was out of control and far too quick to jump on her child. But I remind myself that I am seeing only a snippet of the day. It's not fair to judge without knowing the full story. Maybe her child had been misbehaving all day, and she'd reached the final straw. Maybe the child was being a total asshole, and I didn't see it. Today, the blame has shifted to parents whenever anything goes wrong. I think the story of baby Jessica really drives home how our society has changed.

In 1987 at the age of eighteen months, a young toddler named Jessica fell into a twenty-two-foot deep well in her aunt's backyard. She spent fifty-eight hours trapped in the well before being rescued. Because the well was so tight, it was a huge production to get her out. They brought in cranes and diggers and thousands of people while the whole thing was being broadcast around the world. I read about the incident recently in conjunction with the story about the young boy who fell into the gorilla enclosure at the Cincinnati Zoo.

The journalist who wrote the article about the two events pointed out the difference between the public's reaction then and now. When baby Jessica fell into the well, it was an accident, a tragic accident but one with a happy ending. A little girl had simply been running and exploring in her backyard. There was nothing unusual, just another day in a kid's life. When the young boy fell into the gorilla's enclosure, everyone was quick to jump on the mother. What was she doing? Why wasn't she taking better care of son? Why did she let him out of her sight? I was guilty, too. I thought, *How could a little boy get so far from his mother without her noticing that he fell into a gorilla enclosure?*

I wasn't there, so I don't know what the situation was. Even if the mother was partly to blame, the media was all over her. The reporter's point was that when baby Jessica fell down the well, no one said how horrible her parents were and that they deserved to lose their child, like people say today. No one demanded that Child Protective Services take Jessica out of her home. It was an accident. What changed?

Now the blame is 100 percent on the parents. If something goes wrong with children, it's immediately the parents' fault. I think that has a lot to do with why parents are so unwilling to discipline in public. Parents are judged guilty before anyone knows what happened.

The same is true if you intervene when a child is acting out in a store. The parents are at fault for not having control of their child, or you're criticized if you do something to your kid to prevent things from getting out of hand. You're damned if you do and damned if you don't.

We need to stop being so overly concerned with what other people think and simply deal with our children in the moment. It won't always be comfortable, but there are appropriate ways to handle things.

Most of us have had the experience of being in a restaurant next to a family whose child is misbehaving. It ruins everyone's meal. I want to walk over to the parents and calmly say, "Would you like me to deal with this?"

When one of our kids acts up in a restaurant, I excuse myself with the child and go to the bathroom for a quick conversation. This is the one warning: change your behavior now or we'll be leaving without finishing dinner or having dessert. Then I make sure to ask if he or she understood what I'd said. This is an important part of any parenting discussion. Always ask your child, "Do you understand what I just said?" Nodding is not acceptable. I make sure my child answers with, "Yes, Mom, I understand." If nothing changes after we get back to the table, we pack up the family, pay the bill, and leave. We deal with the punishment outside or in the car. We don't stay in the restaurant and ruin other people's dinner.

Whenever I correct my children's behavior or tell them what they can or can't do, I always make sure they understand and respond to me. I want to know that they've been paying attention. Kids will tune out and just wait for you to shut up. I ask them to repeat what I said and to tell me they understand. They don't have to like it or agree with it, but they do have to understand what I'm saying.

NIP BAD BEHAVIOR IN THE BUD

I was at Walmart with Soleil when she was young. We were in the toy aisle, and I told her that I was happy for her to have a look at the toys, but we weren't going to be getting one that day.

Of course, she saw a toy that she wanted. I reminded her that we weren't getting anything, and she snapped. Soleil was never one to have a tantrum, so I was shocked. She threw herself on the ground in the most dramatic fashion and started screaming and kicking her feet. "Why, Mommy? Why can't I have this? You are so mean." The works. It was actually quite comical. Remembering advice my sister had given me, I didn't acknowledge or engage with Soleil, and I didn't try to calm her down. I just stepped over her and said that when she was finished, I'd be on the other side of the aisle. I took the cart, turned the corner, and stayed there.

Once I was out of sight, Soleil looked up to see where I'd gone. She yelled out to me and looked around the corner, and that was the end of her tantrum. Later, when we were in the car, we talked about her behavior and that I didn't want to see it again. It's not that I avoided dealing with her tantrum. I defused it instead by not feeding into it.

A lot of parents try to stop tantrums and ease bad behavior in stores by feeding into it. Mothers will pull out a lollipop from their purse and hand it to their children to shut them up. They end up rewarding the bad behavior with a treat instead of saying no, pulling the kid aside, and properly disciplining him or her. The same thing will only happen again, and it'll do long-term damage.

The longer you allow bad behavior to continue, the more you'll have to backpedal later to correct it. Deal with the tantrum in the moment so it doesn't become a recurring problem. Soleil never threw another tantrum in a store again. The tantrum simply didn't work with me.

⬦⬦⬦⬦⬦⬦⬦⬦⬦⬦

It Takes a Village

We were at a Christmas party about a year ago in a very nice home. One of my friend's kids was jumping all over the couches and kept knocking over a lamp. The kid was being a shithead.

His parents kept doing the usual parent thing and told him repeatedly to stop and get off the couch. But there was no action behind their words and no threat of repercussions to make the kid stop doing anything.

Eventually, seeing that the furniture was going to get destroyed, I walked over and grabbed the kid by the hand, looked him in the eye, and said that if he didn't get off the couch immediately, he was going to have a problem. He looked at me with the fear of God in his eyes.

Then everything came to a sudden stop in the room. All eyes were on me. There was an awkward moment of silence, as if everyone was thinking to themselves, *You're not his parent; you can't do that!*

From then on, the kid was good, like a normal kid instead of an asshole. I felt weird, though, because it wasn't my house. My friends knew that there are things I won't tolerate from any child, mine or theirs, and being an asshole was one of them. Either they deal with it or I will.

It doesn't benefit kids to let them act like that. If parents keep letting things go, a cop will have to deal with it down the road, or a teacher, or an idiot who's packing a nine millimeter. There's no escaping the fact that someone will have to deal with it.

I didn't care if my friends at the party were mad at me. I knew I'd done the best thing for the kid in the situation.

I believe there's truth in the popular saying that it takes a village to raise a family. If my kid or someone else's is being an asshole and gets out of line, I'm OK with anyone letting them know.

CHAPTER 8

Dude, Your Kid Is on Overload

*Yes, it's important to keep your kids active
and to instill passions and skills, but
don't get too caught up in the hype.*

Having to schedule everything—after-school activities, clubs, sport teams, martial arts, dance—for my three kids is a fucking nightmare. Some days, it seems logistically impossible, with five activities for three kids and two parents who work late into the afternoon. All the running around, though, helped me put things into perspective. There are so many things we want our kids to be a part of and so many things they want to do, but the truth is, they simply can't do it all.

I'm a firm believer in downtime for kids. They need unstructured time to play and unwind. I'm concerned we've gotten away from unorganized activity when kids are free to simply play.

When we were living abroad, the kids were especially over-scheduled. On Monday, Tuesday, and Thursday, they had swimming after school; on Tuesday, Wednesday, and Friday, there was dance. Weekends were for clubs and whatever else parents could squeeze into the schedule. Trying to arrange an after-school playdate required a calendar. At school, the kids had a short recess and a lunch break, but there was no time to decompress. When school ended, we shuttled them to one of their scheduled activities. Once we were home, they were expected to do their homework and school projects with the same energy they'd had at the start of the day.

Unless we let kids play, relax, and simply be, they'll get overloaded. The same is true for adults. We all need time to unwind at the end of the day, whether it's having a hot bath after work or sitting in front of the TV for an hour. But when it comes to our kids, we want them entertained all the time. Even stay-at-home moms opt to leave their kids in after-school care until five o'clock in order to have a few more hours in the day for themselves and let someone else keep their kids busy. Day care and after-school care have become overused by people who don't need them. Those services are for parents who work, not a mother or father who wants a few extra hours for themselves. It points to the problem of expecting our children to be entertained all the time.

We've come to believe that our kids need lots of things to do after school or we're not doing a good job of parenting them. We feel the need to immerse them in every activity. What happened to coming home from school and riding a bike around the neighborhood, playing outside, or coloring? What's wrong with letting our kids relax and veg out in front of the computer or TV for an hour? If kids are constantly busy, there's no time for them to be creative and use their imaginations. Let them get their hands dirty, build something outside, or paint, and don't worry about the mess you'll have to clean up later!

When we tell our boys that it's time to disconnect from their computers, first we get the shit face, followed by "There's nothing else to do" or "I just want to finish my round." But with a little direction, their creativity soon kicks in. They dump their Lego bin and start building, or pull the cushions off the couch for a Nerf war. They are free to explore and use their brains in new ways and, best of all, have fun.

Of course, your kid may truly love to play sports, go to chess club, and play the piano. Many kids do. My niece is like that with dance. She dances competitively and practices four or five times a week for a couple of hours each day. But sometimes with homework, trying to fit in a social life, and being part of her family on top of dance practice, the stress takes its toll and makes her cry. It's important to find the right balance, and whatever it is your kid loves to do, make sure to keep it fun.

EVERYTHING HAS A FUCKING SHOE

I don't want to imply that I don't support extracurricular activities. Our boys do jiu-jitsu and mixed martial arts, and our daughter dances and plays the violin. I want my children to learn outside of the classroom, too. We're a fitness family and want our kids to stay active and be involved in sports. It's good for their bodies as well as their minds and social skills. Many social skills are learned best by being part of a team or group, and that includes the good shit that happens in the locker room, on team trips, and in competitions. Some of Aaron's favorite stories from when he played soccer come from the locker room. They are priceless life experiences.

I also believe that too much activity creates asshole kids. And you can't blame the kids. They're tired, overstimulated, and often stressed out. With too much on their plates, they become irritable and have little patience. A bad cycle of being overtired and behaving badly sets in, and we're the ones to blame. We created the chaos in the first place by overloading the kids' schedule with too much crap.

We used to haul around what was lovingly referred to as "the bag." Maybe you have one in your car, too. It was full of shoes and equipment for every activity my kids were doing—hockey shoes, soccer cleats, and four types of dance shoes for Soleil. Everything needed its own fucking shoe! I put the shoes plus uniforms, mouth guards, tutus, and tights in a big blue canvas sports bag and stuck it in the back of the car so that we always had everything we needed with us.

One day, it hit me as I was hauling the big bag around. I asked myself whether they really needed to be doing all those activities.

It was time for an intervention. I was exhausted keeping the schedules straight, driving from school to field to dance studio, and stressing if we'd make it on time. So we sat down and focused on what each kid really wanted to do. If they answered my simple question about whether they loved the sport or not with no, we eliminated it. We ended up with a schedule that, although still busy, works for all of us, and I know the kids love what they're doing. As for the bag? It no longer exists.

TIME TO HANG OUT WITH FAMILY

At the end of each day, we try to come together as a family. We're not always able to sit down and have dinner together because we have a lot of moving parts, but we do feel it's important to connect with each kid at the end of the day. We either come together in the living room to catch up, or Aaron and I visit each kid and share some time with them.

Some of my favorite moments happen when I least expect it. As part of Kesler's bedtime routine, we read a story. Because he's only four, he likes Curious George or Little Critter or something similar. Often when I am reading to him, Soleil and Everest will wander in and jump into bed to listen. It's not that they're interested in the book; they just want to be a part of the moment, and it always makes my heart explode when they do. The fact that a ten- and thirteen-year-old still want to jump in bed with their mom and little brother to listen to a child's story tells me that we may be doing something right. I cherish those moments.

You can easily miss out on those special moments if you don't take time to slow down and connect. If you're always running around picking up kids from swimming lessons or dance, you aren't leaving room for the small but significant connections to occur, which happen spontaneously when everyone is available. If kids' schedules are overloaded, there's no time available to simply hang out.

When Soleil was born, friends would tell me to "enjoy it now because time goes by fast." When you're knee-deep in newborns, feedings, and diapers with no sleep, it's easy to wish for things to get easier and the first phase to be over. Or at least I did. But childhood is short, which I realize even more now that my children are getting older. I find myself trying to hold on to each moment and creating opportunities to stay connected with my kids before their friends become a bigger priority than me.

Give yourself and your kids time to have fun and enjoy life as a family.

◇◇◇◇◇◇◇◇◇

Four-Hour School Days in Norway

The other day, Liz and I read that Norway has been testing a new school system. They're sending their kids to school for only four hours a day. They've discovered that the kids are learning just as much as when they spent eight hours in school. In fact, grades went up when the school day got shorter.

I recently saw another report based in the United States that found no scientific evidence supporting homework in grades ten and lower.

The concept of an eight-hour school day is based on a myth. Humans function best when they have an equal amount of time to learn, rest, relax, and play. It's our goal that our kids have as much time to play and relax as they do for learning. I think those two findings prove the point.

I believe in balance. I don't think it's healthy to force your kid to be an athlete, musician, straight-A student, volunteer, and Nobel Prize winner all at once. Usually when that happens, you'll find an insecure asshole parent who feels he or she comes up short.

CHAPTER 9

Fuck the Participation Trophy

We all want our kids to be winners, but sometimes you have to lose to learn to win.

As a person who loves sports and competition, I find that one of the most painful developments in parenting in recent years is the belief that every kid is a winner. Of course, we all believe our children are unique and wonderful, but when it comes to competition, there will always be winners and losers, both on and off the field.

It's important for children to understand that in all situations, there will be people who succeed and others who fail, whether at a sporting event, at school, or at the office when they grow up. How a person handles winning or losing reveals a lot about who he or she is. We all need to learn how to win and lose graciously.

When Everest and Soleil were young, their school sponsored a Terry Fox Run to benefit the Canadian Cancer Society. Terry Fox is a Canadian hero. He was the first person in Canada to run cross-country for cancer research in the 1970s. He was young at the time and had already lost a leg to cancer. At that time, a prosthetic limb was little more than a metal bar with a shoe on the end. Despite the weather, pain, and his illness, Terry ran across Canada, capturing the hearts of Canadians. Now the Terry Fox Run is an annual event in many countries around the world.

The year Everest was in kindergarten, both Soleil and Everest participated, and I went to school to watch the race. The kids who were good runners were at the head of the pack, and the young boy who won crossed the finish line well ahead of the other kids. He was clearly a natural runner. I'd seen him in other cross-country competitions. He was a gazelle. It was no surprise that he'd be first to finish. When he crossed the line, he was handed a purple participation ribbon, and each child who came in after him was also given exactly the same purple ribbon.

In the past, they'd always awarded first- through tenth-place ribbons to the kids who crossed the finish line first and participation ribbons to the rest of the runners. That year, they did things differently, and every kid got the same participation ribbon. The boy who had won the race had expected a white first-place ribbon and stood there perplexed as everyone who crossed the line received the same purple ribbon. He was clearly disappointed, and rightly so, even though he didn't complain. I was impressed. If I'd been him, I'd probably have pitched a fucking fit about not being acknowledged as first.

I felt so bad for him that I went to my car and looked for something to reward him with—a piece of chocolate or anything to say I'd noticed that he'd kicked some ass out there. All I found was a $5 bill, which I gave to him. I told him I was sorry he wasn't getting any recognition for being the winner and that I wanted him to buy himself an ice-cream cone to celebrate and be rewarded for all his effort. He wasn't looking for a lot of fanfare; he just wanted the special ribbon that he'd earned. If I'd have had more money that day, I'd have showered the first ten kids with dollar bills like a young man in the front row of a strip show. Instead, an opportunity to teach a valuable life lesson was lost.

LEARNING TO LOSE

The Olympics set a good example. Nobody cares who comes in fourth at the Olympics, even if it's only by a hundredth of a second. Only the gold, silver, and bronze medalists count and receive sponsorships and endorsement contracts. They have the opportunity for the course of their lives to be altered by their win. Has anyone seen Nike sponsor an Olympian who was close to getting the bronze medal? Whether we like it or not, the world celebrates winners, and in order to have a winner, there has to be a loser.

We can end up giving our kids the wrong message when we don't recognize and celebrate winners. Do we really want our kids to think they don't have to work harder than anyone else because in the end, they'll all get the same ribbon? I don't believe kids should be rewarded simply for participating. That's what kids do anyway. There was no option for not participating in the Terry Fox Run unless a child was hurt or ill. We're patting kids on the back for fucking showing up! I believe that teaches them two things: no effort is needed for acknowledgment (which is bullshit), and there's no point in making an effort if it'll be overlooked anyway.

Your kids are not going to like losing. Who does? They will cry, be upset, and make excuses for their lack of success. Like most things, it's a learned behavior. If our kids get upset because they aren't wining, it's our fault as parents.

We have to teach kids how to lose gracefully. Losing is an opportunity for a teachable moment: if you want to win, you have to work harder. Aaron and I always tell our kids it's OK to lose. Losing, like failure, is an opportunity to evaluate what went wrong and grow from the mistake. Poor losers, whether they're kids or adults, look like assholes.

Losing naturally doesn't sit well for any of us. I used to play competitive volleyball and field hockey as a teen. Our field hockey league was highly competitive, and although we were a good team, we were never the best. My dad used to try to get under my skin when I came home from a game we'd lost by saying, "Second place is the first loser." It used to make me furious, but in hindsight, there's truth to what he said.

My husband's sister is eight years younger than him. She's has an incredible voice and sings with a local band in Vancouver, British Columbia. They're popular and play at parties and weddings.

Once, his sister entered a singing competition and placed second, although I personally thought she sang better than the girl who won. After the competition was over, his sister came over to where we were sitting. She, of course, was disappointed she hadn't won and had an excuse for all the reasons why—the judge was a friend of the girl who won, the contestants weren't able to choose their own songs, another singer was given better songs to sing, and so on.

After a while, Aaron stopped her and told her that those weren't the reasons why she'd lost. She lost, he said, because the other singer was better. It was as simple as that. It was a hard pill for her to swallow, but it was the truth.

There are no excuses for losing, although we can be critical of our efforts and wished we'd done better. However, using another person's success as an excuse for our own failure, or that of our kids, is never right. Inspire your kids to do better. Ask them why they think they lost and what could they do differently the next time. Teach them accountability for their actions.

CELEBRATE THE VICTORIES

Soleil is not a natural runner, but she likes to run. The first time she qualified in cross-country running for a citywide meet of independent schools she placed thirteenth. They gave ribbons to the first twenty winners, so she got a thirteen-place ribbon and was so proud of herself.

The next year before the race, I asked Soleil what she was aiming for, and she said she wanted to go for twelfth. *Great*, I thought, *she wants to do better than she did the previous year*. Even though Soleil recognized her running skills would not likely put her in first place, she set a goal to better her placement from the previous year. In her eyes, that was a win. She ended up placing tenth, which she was thrilled about. She'd exceeded her expectations.

Being competitive doesn't mean your kids have to be an asshole about wanting to be first all the time. A competitive spirit is wanting to do better each time. Soleil was realistic. She knew who she was up against and was honest in her assessment of what she could achieve. It was a victory, and we celebrated it like one.

Even if your child doesn't win first or second place, it's important to celebrate his or her victories. Having winners and losers doesn't mean you can't celebrate your child coming in fifth. Children need to take pride for being in fifth place, otherwise they won't want to try for first place the next time. If you belittle fifth place and treat it with negativity, your child will see it in the same way and become a sore loser. Celebrate the small victories because each small victory leads to a bigger one.

LEARNING TO WIN

Just as important as knowing how to lose graciously is winning graciously. It's great to celebrate being number one with your kids. We love it when our kids are the best. However, there's a fine line between gloating and celebrating.

Every kid deserves his or her moment in the spotlight. Kids should be proud of what they've earned. Celebrating your kids' successes gives them confidence and makes them eager to continue moving forward, especially when they're passionate about what they're doing. There's never any need to be sorry or apologize for being the best when they've put in the effort.

At the same time, you want to discourage gloating and inflating an ego until it becomes unmanageable. Like making excuses for losing, being an overconfident winner also makes a kid look like an asshole. There's a balance between the two. You want your kids to celebrate their success without their ego getting out of control.

We always tell our kids that when we compete, no matter how great we may be at something, there's a good chance there'll be somebody who's even better. That's simply the way things are. You may be the best runner in Canada, but it's a big world and good runners are everywhere. There aren't many Usain Bolts in the world and even he has his competition.

Kids should own their success but not become so self-absorbed that they think they can do no wrong. Life will always provide a challenge. It may sound harsh, but you should prepare your kids for disappointments. Few people reach the point in their life when they're the best in the world in their sport or field. And even if they do, there will always be another "best" right behind them. They will have to keep working hard each day to improve their skills and prove that they are the best for as long as they can.

A good example is in the Ultimate Fighting Championship (UFC). If you're not a fight fan, you may not know about the UFC, which involves two men fighting with a mix of martial arts and boxing in an octagon. I love the sport, but it's definitely not for the weak of heart. There are knockouts, blood, and big testosterone-steroid-pumping fucking egos. It's a game about who can make the most money in the shortest amount of time. There are always one or two superstars who have the skills to be the champ and the ego to please the crowd. They ride the wave of success for a while, but as they age, they take a few more hits to the head. The next generation of fighters comes along, and the superstars' time at the top begins to be riddled with defeats. The stars lose their shine and others take their place. That's how it goes. We all have to make the most of our time to shine and understand that we'll be sharing the spotlight with someone new sooner or later. How we step aside, ideally with grace and class, defines who we are as a person.

In our house, we live by the familiar saying that "if you talk the talk, then you have to walk the walk." If you say you're the best, then you have to follow it up with your actions. If not, you look like a blowhole who can't follow up on his promises.

We have many friends in Texas, where the football culture is incredibly competitive. Boys start playing as young as five. One of our friends coaches a football team for young boys aged six to eight. The first time I went to watch one of their games, I was amazed at their competitiveness at such a young age. At the end of the year, there's a round robin competition. The teams come together and play in divisions based on how many wins and losses they had during the year. The top teams play one another, the middle teams play with other middle teams, and so on. There's a winner in each division.

In my friend's league, they decided to change the rules and not award first-, second-, and third-place trophies. They felt the trophies put too much emphasis on winning, and they already had a bad reputation for being too competitive.

That year, every team received a participation trophy, no matter which division they were in or how they finished. Our friend's team was in the top division. During the ceremonies at the end of the competition when his team was handed their participation trophies, he thanked the officials, took a bag, collected every boy's trophy, and handed the bag back to the league manager.

He explained that his team wouldn't be accepting their trophies because they had placed fourth and wouldn't have gotten a trophy in other circumstances. They hadn't played well enough to earn a trophy.

A lot of parents from the team were angry, but I thought it was fucking amazing. Our friend didn't want to teach the boys that they get a trophy even if they'd played poorly and weren't all that great. It wasn't OK to be rewarded for playing the worst they'd ever played, and it also wasn't OK to not recognize those teams that had worked hard and played really well.

It created a big controversy at the time and was covered in the newspapers. Because of all the media coverage, the league went back to awarding trophies only to the teams that came in first, second, and third.

Kids aren't weaklings. They're not so sensitive that they can't withstand coming in fourth place. That's how the "pussification" of children started. We make our kids into giant pussies because we don't want them to feel bad for losing, which is ridiculous because the world doesn't work that way whether it's on the field, in the office, or in romance. It's always about competition, whether we want to admit it or not. Why do we try to make it easy for kids and pat them on the back for whatever effort they make?

Not everyone will get the same pay and the same big office. We're not rewarded for merely showing up to our jobs every day. That's not how the world works. There are always winners and losers. That's why billions of dollars are spent on events like the Olympics, the Super Bowl, and the Stanley Cup. People want to see a winner and a loser. We have to teach our kids that it's OK to be both. We won't do irreparable damage to their egos if we let them lose. Otherwise, when they grow up, it'll be a shock to realize that success requires effort.

Everest's Soccer Tryouts

I used to play soccer at the highest level in Canada. I was a goalkeeper, played for the provincial team, and was invited to the national soccer development center. Unfortunately, I stopped growing. Goalkeepers are typically about six foot four. I'm five foot ten. They gave me the bad news, and that was it. I was nineteen at the time and started doing mixed martial arts full time instead.

Given my good soccer DNA, I put Everest into soccer when he was a little boy, but he didn't love it. He didn't like being cold and wet all the time. After a year, he decided to do jiu-jitsu instead, which was fine with me. Just because I was good at soccer didn't mean he had to do the same thing, which is how a lot of dads think.

Out of the blue when we were living in the Cayman Islands, which is a huge soccer country, Everest came to me and said he wanted to try out for the school's soccer team.

While all the rest of his classmates were running around playing soccer, he'd been playing make-believe or *Minecraft* games with his buddy. Soccer wasn't his thing, so I was surprised that he wanted to try out.

I asked him what position he wanted to play, and he said he was going for goalie. *OK*, I thought, *he never plays soccer; all these kids are supercompetitive and good; they play every day, every recess, and every lunch hour; and of all positions, he wants to try for the one position he can't hide in. As a goalie, he will be constantly exposed.*

My heart didn't want him to do it; he'd just embarrass himself. My head said to let him do it and support him. In our house, we believe that not only will failure happen, but you should also embrace it and fail as fast as possible. The only way anything good ever happens is when trying something new and learning. The best way to learn is to fail, so we encourage failure—to fail forward and as fast as possible.

Everest and I went out to buy cleats and the other gear. Goalie is the one position in soccer that needs the most equipment. The gloves alone go for a hundred bucks. All the time we were shopping, I was thinking to myself about all the money I was spending and that the stuff would be used only one time. What a waste! But I'd made the commitment.

I proposed to Everest that we practice together. I'd show him some things, even though, of course, you can't teach someone how to play a complicated position in three days. Finally, the tryout day arrived, and Everest was fired up.

He actually did pretty well. Although he's a bit soft, he's got a fearless streak in him. Lots of balls were pinged off him, and he made some saves. He couldn't kick because he'd had no practice. Every time he had to kick, it was terrible. He didn't know the rules because he hadn't played the game in years, so when it was time for a goal kick, he had no idea what to do. But to his credit, he didn't let in a single goal.

Twenty-two players showed up for the tryouts, five of them wanting to be goalkeepers, and they were going to take only thirteen kids for the team. At most, they'd take one full-time goalie and one backup. The five who wanted to be goalie were all much bigger, more athletic, and more experienced than Everest. But it didn't stop him from going out there and doing his best. I was superproud of him because he played well even if he didn't have the skills.

At the end of the tryouts, the coach announced he'd let everyone know in three days' time who made the team and who didn't. Everest was sure he was going to make the team because he hadn't let in any goals. I didn't know if he was confident or delusional. When he went to school for the results, the coach said to him that if the selection had been about heart alone, Everest would be first on the team. He'd played great, but he wasn't quite there in other ways. Everest needed to practice more.

Everest came home and told me the results without crying. Then suddenly he burst into tears and started going on about how he hadn't let in a single goal, that he was the best and should have been picked, and that the coach didn't know what he was talking about. Here was a teachable moment. I could have simply said that that's what happens sometimes, or I could make the most of the situation.

It hurt me, but I told Everest that he wasn't the best goalkeeper or the second best, third best, or fourth best. "Everest," I said, "you were the fifth best goalkeeper who tried out that day."

I also told him that it wasn't because he hadn't tried hard that he didn't make the team and that I was so proud of him. I explained that in order to be good at something, you have to do it a lot. You have to be passionate about it, and you have to do it all the time. Every one of the other boys plays soccer and practices every day and that simply makes them better. If he wanted to be on the team, he could be, but it wouldn't be by walking into a tryout after deciding the week before and practicing for only six hours that he could expect to make the team. It wasn't realistic. It was no one's fault, and it wasn't political. He simply was the fifth best goalkeeper that day.

Everest understood. Then I asked him what he wanted to do. How badly did he want to play soccer? Was it a passing thing, or was he serious about it? If he was serious, I told him, I'd work with him and make him the best goalkeeper in the country. I had the knowledge to do it, but Everest had to put in the work. It was up to him to decide whether he wanted to earn it like everyone else. In the end, he decided against it. He wasn't that interested in soccer. It was more of a fad, and that's fine. But to allow him to believe that he'd gotten screwed over was not going to benefit him later in life. He now knows that whatever it is he wants, it will have to be earned.

That's why I say, fuck the participation trophy.

CHAPTER 10

Keeping It Real with Your Kids

———

Your kid has questions. Don't bullshit him.

Baby talk is one of my biggest pet peeves. It's natural, of course, to want to sweet talk newborns. We love to coo at them, make silly sounds, and coddle them, but after the age of one, you need to cut out that shit. When I see parents talking to their five-year-old like he was an idiot, I want to scratch my eyes out. Give your kids more credit than that. Once children can speak, they're little sponges, absorbing whatever comes their way, including, "Did you make poo-poo today?" WTF?

Baby talk is talking to your kids like they're stupid, which they're not. It stunts their emotional growth and is detrimental to language development. All three of my children started speaking at a young age. Parents talk down to kids because they assume kids don't understand what they're saying when in fact children's comprehension is far greater than we give them credit for.

Studies say that children's brains from the time they're born to three years of age crave information. It's the prime time for children to learn a musical instrument or multiple languages. We North Americans don't do a great job of taking advantage of that window of opportunity when our kids are young. They're capable of absorbing much more than we think.

We have good friends who live in the Caribbean. When their son was four, he was already speaking three languages fluently. They're a multicultural family. Mom is from Sweden, dad is German, and English was the primary language where they were living. They can converse with their son in any one of those languages, and he responds. A child's brain has huge potential, so there's no need to baby our kids. I understand letting kids be kids and enjoy their childhood. I want the same thing for my children, but kids can play and learn at the same time.

Kids will follow your example. People frequently comment to me about how clearly my kids speak. They say they sound so grown up for their age, especially Kesler, who's only five and has a large vocabulary. That's because we don't dumb down the words we use to suit what we *think* is his capacity for understanding. We ask him if he understands everything and whether there's a word he doesn't know. If there is, we'll have created an opportunity to teach him something new. It may not stick the first time he hears it, but in time, he learns a new big word.

I often hear Kesler repeat what he's heard. We like to use the word *appropriate* a lot, and I've heard Kesler say to his brother, "Everest, that's not appropriate." It's funny coming from a five-year-old even though I know he's heard the word repeated so often in our house that he's picked it up. Now he can use *appropriate* in the right context. It shows that kids are capable of learning a lot more than we expect. The same holds true for words we don't wish our children to use. I'm now having to censor myself when my kids are around!

Teaching vocabulary to your kids gives them a strong base for expressing themselves. And when they don't understand something, they can ask what it means, which is a good thing. By taking advantage of teachable moments, you help your kids to stretch up rather than you dumbing down.

HOW MUCH INFORMATION IS TOO MUCH?

As I mentioned in chapter 4, I used to watch the *Supernanny* TV show as a sideline parent. A sideline parent, as most of us know, is the person who has no kids but is quick to tell parents what they're doing wrong or how to do things better.

One thing Supernanny said that has always stuck with me is that whenever your kids ask a question, provide only enough information to satisfy their curiosity. If they continue asking questions, then you know the information you gave them wasn't enough and you need to elaborate. Her theory, which I agree with, is that the answers you provide have to be age appropriate. What you may think is a big question from your five-year-old may not need a big answer because he or she doesn't have the worldly experience for more than the basics.

As an example, Aaron was raised mostly by a single mom. When he was five years old, she filled him in on everything there was to know about girls getting their period. He'd asked her a question about a tampon box he'd seen in the bathroom, and she felt that she had to give him a complete answer. She launched into a discussion of the fallopian tubes and everything else, which burned itself into Aaron's brain at the age of five and was probably way too much information.

We've had the same question at our house from the boys.

We start with giving a basic answer. When Kesler asked me what tampons were, I said they were something for ladies to use in the bathroom and stopped to see what he would say. He replied, "OK, well, I'm not a lady," and that was it.

I didn't tell him anything that was untrue. I gave him only enough information to satisfy his curiosity. Had he asked another question, I would have elaborated and gone to the next step, but he didn't. I knew then that that was all he wanted to know.

Everest, on the other hand, is almost ten and is more curious about things like that. He'll ask more in-depth questions, but I expect that at his age. I'll elaborate more when I answer his questions until the same thing happens. Either he loses interest, or he keeps asking questions. There's a balance between giving your kids too much information and not enough. I think you have to stop when the questions stop. There's no need to overdo it.

When Soleil was about six years old, she used to sleep-walk a lot—not to the point where she'd unlock the front door and go outside, but she'd wander around the house. It was nerve-racking for me because the house we lived in at the time had a large double staircase, and I was concerned that she was going to fall down the stairs in the middle of the night.

It was like Soleil was in a trance when she sleepwalked. Her eyes were open, and if you didn't know that she was asleep, you'd think she was just roaming around the house. She was quite alert for sleepwalking. It used to freak the shit out of me because it was so eerie.

One night, Aaron and I were in bed having sex, and we didn't realize that Soleil had walked into the room. She came up to the side of the bed and just stood there. I'm not sure how long she'd been there before we noticed her, so God knows what she witnessed. I think I actually screamed when I turned and saw her staring at us. She had no expression on her face whatsoever and calmly said, "I need a snack."

It was about 1:00 a.m., and I knew she was half-awake and half-asleep. Of course, I was in a panic, thinking, *Oh my God, she's seen us having sex. What am I going to say to her?* I got up and quietly shuffled her back to bed, and she fell right back to sleep. But I didn't sleep the rest of the night because I was thinking about how I was going to approach the subject of parents having sex with a six-year-old.

I'd heard so many horror stories from friends about when they had walked in on their parents having sex, and how they'd never forget it. It didn't happen to me as a kid, but now it had just happened to me as the parent.

All the next morning, I kept waiting for Soleil to ask me what had been going on the night before, but she didn't. Obviously, she'd been asleep and not quite conscious enough to know what she was seeing. At one point, I thought I should bring it up but then realized she wasn't asking, so I wasn't going to tell. If it had registered and she'd been disturbed or curious by what she'd seen, she would have asked me. I wasn't going to offer the information because I needed to clear the air for myself. Obviously, nothing seemed unusual to her.

This is a good example of knowing when not to offer information that's not needed and waiting for the question to be asked. You have to find the right balance between your kids' maturity level and holding back information. Provide enough information for their age level but no more. There's no need to go into every single detail if kids aren't old enough to understand.

BEING OPEN WITH KIDS

Aaron's mom was more of a free spirit and open to talking about sex than my parents were. I don't remember ever seeing my parents in their underwear, let alone naked. As I grew older, it bothered me that I felt insecure about my body and nakedness when I was growing up. Aaron and I wanted to find the middle ground as parents.

When our kids were young, we had what I'd call a naked household. Not that we'd wander around naked all the time, but we didn't want our kids to feel strange or uncomfortable if they walked in on anyone who was naked.

The boys are happy to be naked. For Kesler, especially, part of it has to do with growing up in the Caribbean where it's hot all the time; he's cooler being naked.

Everest is very confident in his body. If we're in the bathroom together and he wants to jump in the shower, he'll take off his shorts midconversation in front of me. He doesn't even think about it. And vice versa if he walks in and I've just gotten out of the shower, I don't feel the need to grab a towel.

Whereas Soleil, who's nearly a teenager, is becoming more self-conscious of her body and doesn't like changing clothes when the boys are in her room. She's very conscious of her nakedness. We respect that it makes her uncomfortable and do our best not to go naked around her. It's normal that she's more aware of everyone's body now.

If you're not open with your children about their bodies and sex, they'll search for the information elsewhere. It's naïve to think they won't. Things have changed since we grew up. When I was a kid, I had two options if I wanted to know something about sex. I could go to the library to look for a book about sex and read it secretly (I'd have been too embarrassed if I'd gotten caught reading it openly). The other option was to go to the corner store where the owner didn't care who bought *Hustler* or *Playboy* magazines and read about sex that way. I did both.

Now the availability of information on the Internet is crazy. If they can spell it, kids can find it on Google, both the good and the bad. What's on TV continues to surprise me, too. What used to be late-night programming is now on all the time. I'm finding I have to monitor age-appropriate programs at 7:00 p.m.! We live by the rule that if our kids come to us with honest questions, we give them honest answers, even if it's uncomfortable for us.

When Everest was seven, he ended up on a porn site. We had one iPad at the time and took turns using it. Everest used to take it up to his room. At a certain point when I told him his time was up, he asked for extra time to shut everything down. I never gave it much thought until one day, he gave me the iPad and when I opened the search engine, a porn site came up.

I thought it was weird but didn't connect the dots at first, maybe because I didn't want to face the fact that Everest was potentially watching porn. A couple of days later after he'd borrowed my phone, I noticed when I was looking for something, that the same site was on my search engine. Curious, I clicked to check it out. Holy shit! I discovered some serious, aggressive, hard-core porn. There was nothing good about the site.

I went into a complete panic: *Oh, my God, my baby's been watching this stuff for at least a week!* Frantic and not knowing what to do, I went to Aaron and told him what had happened. I would have been comfortable dealing with Everest and talking with him about the site but felt it could potentially embarrass him. I figured Aaron and Everest had the same equipment, so it was better his dad speak with him. He could have questions about his penis, which is more of a dad-and-son discussion.

To be honest, I have no problem with porn. I'm not here to judge what gets people off, but when your seven-year-old is watching hard-core porn, it's a serious issue.

We'd never talked to Everest about sex, so we were faced with a choice. Either he was going to get in trouble for what he'd been doing or we'd use the situation as a teachable moment. We agreed there was no reason to punish him because he was just being curious.

Aaron went up to Everest's room, and they ended up having an amazing and honest conversation about sex and relationships. Aaron explained to him that what he'd seen on the iPad wasn't what love looks like and was meant to be shocking. It wasn't what a relationship between a man and a woman really is. Everest had lots of questions, of course, mostly about his own body. They were all natural and normal questions, which made me feel relieved. If he had asked some freaky questions, I would have been very upset.

We could have pretended nothing had happened and buried our head in the sand, hoping Everest wouldn't find the site again if we erased it from the history. If we hadn't confronted the situation head-on, he would have either continued looking for similar material on his own or tried to find it from someone else, and then there was a good chance he wouldn't have gotten the right kind of information. If we had ignored the situation, he could have continued to believe that what he'd watched was normal between a man and a woman, which would have been more damaging in the long run. Creating a good boy comes with the additional responsibility of creating a good man who knows how to treat a woman well.

The issue never came up again because we'd addressed Everest's concerns appropriately. We answered all his questions. We didn't hide anything from him, and we didn't make him feel ashamed or embarrassed. It was all totally new for him. We also established trust between us so that he could come to us with any questions he had about anything in the future. He didn't feel we were judging him.

This "oh shit!" moment turned into a positive, healthy opportunity for growth.

If you have boys, you'll quickly learn that everything becomes about the penis. Aaron had another penis encounter with Everest, but it's a funny story this time.

Aaron occasionally gets a bad case of eczema. It's actually more like psoriasis and is brought on by stress. He gets it in strange places, like his eyelids and on the folds of his ears. And he also gets it on his penis.

One day when he was standing naked in the bathroom shaving, Everest came in. He liked to watch Aaron shave. It's a man thing, and he wants to learn how to do it. Again, he was about seven at the time. He looked at Aaron's penis and said, "Gross, Dad, what's wrong with your penis?" Aaron looked down and said he had a rash and explained to him what it was and when it happens.

Everest was concerned that the same thing would happen to his penis. It led to a larger conversation about body parts and his penis and how it functions. Aaron felt good about the conversation because it established trust. If Everest ever felt there was something wrong with his body or his penis, he could go to Aaron and tell him. He's comfortable sharing his concerns and how he feels with his dad.

It's important to note that my boys will come to me, too, with penis issues because we've established trust and openness in our home. No subject is off limits if approached with honesty and respect.

TALKING ABOUT SEX

Sooner or later, it'll be time to talk with your kids about sex. If you're a parent who can't talk to your kid about sex, then you need to grow the fuck up. We all want sex, and most of us love having sex. We wait all of our teenage lives to have sex. Most people can't stop thinking about sex and want their kids to be aware of the dangers of sex. So why can't they talk to them about it? The body is a natural part of who we are. I want my kids to be comfortable knowing that at any time they can ask me questions if they're concerned about their bodies or are just curious, and I'll answer them as honestly as possible. Otherwise, they'll learn from anyone or anything that offers the information they're looking for.

I don't want my kids getting answers from their friends who probably don't know any more than they do, or finding a site on the Internet that doesn't give them the correct facts, which ends up causing bigger problems. I don't want my kids walking around with knowledge that's incorrect. I want the information to come from me. I'd much rather broach an uncomfortable topic and give them good information than they get it from a secondary source.

If someone who doesn't know what they're talking about gives your kids information and has a bias one way or the other, they'll pass their opinions on to your children. Unless you arm your kids with honest facts, they'll assume that what they hear from someone else is right and adopt the same beliefs. Would you want someone who is homophobic to talk to your kids about sex between two men or two women?

One of my biggest pet peeves is when people call their children's body parts by stupid names. It's not a "pee-pee" or a "wee-wee"; it's a penis (if you're uncomfortable, start saying penis out loud). Why do we feel the need to make up names for our body parts just because other people may find it inappropriate? I always tell the boys that there's nothing wrong with the word *vagina* if that's what they're talking about. It's no different than calling an ear an ear or a nose a nose.

What's not appropriate is using slang words for body parts. Using foul language is disrespectful of people's bodies. It took my mom a while to adjust to the language we use in our house, because she raised us not to talk about anything having to do with sex or our bodies. The first time she heard Kesler say the word *penis* when he was two, she was taken aback. Granted, she hadn't raised boys, but there was nothing for her to be embarrassed about because that's simply what it was. By teaching your kids the right terminology for their body parts, you instill respect for and comfort with their bodies and other people's bodies.

When we lived in the tropics, swimming was part of the kids' PE program. Once a week, they had swim class, and they changed out of their uniforms and put on their swimsuits in same-gender locker rooms.

One day, Everest came home and told me that many boys in his class wait in line to change in the one changing room because they didn't want to take their pants off in front of everyone. I asked him why he thought that was, and he replied that the boys were embarrassed to show their penis. Then I asked him how he felt, and he said it didn't bother him. He said, "We're all boys, Mom. We all have a penis." I agreed and told him there was nothing to be embarrassed about. I felt he needed confirmation that it was OK to get changed in front of other boys and make sure there wasn't anything wrong with him because he didn't have a problem with it. He thought it was strange that boys would waste their playtime standing in the line so they could have privacy to put on their swimsuits. For me it was a pat-on-the-back moment as a mom. Everest had a comfortable and healthy relationship with his body, and that was a victory.

DEALING WITH RACISM, HOMOSEXUALITY, AND OTHER POLITICALLY CORRECT-RIDDLED TOPICS

For two years Eeshan was Kesler's best friend. Eeshan is half white and half Indian (from India, not First Nations or Native American).

When Kesler first came home talking about his buddy Eeshan, I asked him which kid he was. We were new at the school, and I didn't have everyone's name down yet. He answered that Eeshan was kind of small, had brown hair, and had a mark (a birthmark) on his face. I still wasn't sure and asked for more details. The very last thing Kesler mentioned was that Eeshan was brown.

I was struck that he hadn't said that he was brown when I first asked him what Eeshan looked like. He described everything else first. It hadn't occurred to Kesler to say that his friend was brown.

Children are born pure, like a blank canvas. They are not born hating, a racist, or knowing to segregate. I feel fortunate that my children went to an international school for two years. There were seventy-five countries represented at the school and kids of every color, size, and language. It was great exposure to many different cultures.

Kids don't see color when they make friends. They may be curious, but they don't judge it. Children have to be taught to hate, judge, and be cruel. Those are learned behaviors. Ask yourself what you're teaching your child through your generalizations and stereotypes.

Eventually, Kesler asked me why Eeshan was brown. I explained that Eeshan's dad was brown because he was from India, and that most people who live in India have brown skin. Simple!

The language you use when you talk to your kids about race, homosexuality, or transgender is what matters. Transgender is a big topic in our house right now, so it's important that we supply the correct information and use the right words. I never want to pass on racial discrimination through language, even if unintentionally.

My grandmother was one of the most unintentionally racist persons I ever knew. Her language was terrible. It wasn't that she disliked any particular race, but she referred to races in shocking ways. She'd say things like, "Some slant-eye cut me off today while I was driving" or "There sure are a lot of colored folk on TV these days." The first time I heard her say something like that I nearly spit out my food. I told her that she couldn't say things like that in this day and age and that she needed to learn to be more politically correct. Even if it was the way she spoke when she was young, she couldn't keep saying those things. It was hard for her to change. Those were words she'd learned when she grew up. She wasn't saying them in hate, but that was no excuse to keep using them, especially in front of my kids.

It's important to never punish your kids for asking questions. They're simply curious. There are so many different types of people and lifestyles today. I want my kids to feel they can talk to me about any of it. Soleil follows a young woman on YouTube who's a transgender teen trying to raise awareness about transgender issues. I admire her for putting herself out there for an important cause, and Soleil is inspired by her courage. Everest finds it confusing how someone can be born a boy and become a girl, and understandably so. For him, being transgender is an ongoing conversation. He has lots of questions, which is fine. I give him as much information as I can so that it's not foreign to him.

At the risk of being dogmatic, I feel strongly that if you're uncomfortable with homosexuality, you need to find a way to deal with it. Whether or not you agree with their life choices, you need to come to terms with the fact that the gay and lesbian community is not going to disappear. Discomfort breeds fear, and fear breeds hate, so don't pass your fear and hate on to your children. Give them the knowledge they need to make their own decisions.

In our house, love is love, whether it's a man loving a man or a woman loving a woman. That may not be acceptable in every home, especially when there's a strong religious orientation. We have friends who are very religious and for them, homosexuality is a sin. Because we don't share their beliefs, we've had to explain to our kids that religion may play a part in the way some people feel about the gay and lesbian community.

We don't follow any one particular religion, which is not to say we aren't spiritual or believe in a higher being. We live our lives as good people and believe in acceptance for all, no matter the color of your skin, your sexual preference, or your gender. No matter how uncomfortable you may feel, it's so important to establish those positive opinions in your kids when they are young.

If my grandmother at the age of ninety can change her verbiage and my mom, who'll turn seventy next year, can change her conservative perspective on the transgender community, then we should all be able to teach our young children to be tolerant.

⬦⬦⬦⬦⬦⬦⬦⬦⬦⬦

The Penis High Five

When Everest was four, at an age that he was old enough to talk but still incoherent in a funny, sweet kind of way, Liz took Soleil out for a girl date (which is something we encourage all parents do—take your kids out one on one so that they feel special and get alone time with their parents). I told Everest we'd have a man date. We'll do man stuff.

He thought it was an awesome idea. I asked him what we should do first, and he said, "Have a man dinner." Fantastic. Up to the kitchen we went. Then I asked him what kind of food do men eat. He thought about it for a moment and then said, "Hot dogs, pickles, and blueberries." That sounded like a man kind of dinner to me, so that's what we had.

When we were done with dinner, I asked Everest what we should do next on our man date. He said we should go down to the fire pit in our yard, start a fire, and burn some stuff. I told him that sounded like a manly thing to me, so we went down to the fire pit and started the fire with wood we collected around the property.

Eventually, he got tired of that and said he was done.

We walked back up to the house, and I said, "What do you want to do next, buddy?" He said, "I think we should have a man bath." OK, that sounded cool. I went upstairs, started the bath, and put in some bubbles. He got naked and told me to get in, too. I took off my clothes and straddled the raised claw-foot bathtub to get in when Everest looked at me and said, "Dad, I love your giant penis."

I was halfway into the tub and stopped dead in my tracks, thinking to myself, *What did he just say?* He was looking at me with these big eyes and an expression on his face of so much love for his dad. I thought there was nothing I could say that wouldn't be awkward or weird, so I just looked at him and said, "Thanks, buddy," and got in the tub.

We were playing in the bath, and then Everest looked at me and said, "Dad, let's do a penis high five."

"What?" I asked, and Everest said, "You know, like with our hands but with our penises."

"OK, buddy, no problem."

We stood up, and he grabbed his little tiny penis and I grabbed mine, we high-fived them together, and sat back down. Everest was stoked. Then I got him in his pajamas.

It's one of the funniest stories I know. I've told it on stage at seminars to break the ice, and everyone bursts out laughing.

Kids do say weird things, but they're only weird in our context, not theirs.

I was having a shower with Kesler a couple of years later, when he was only two. I soaped him, and he soaped me. I got shampoo in my eyes, so I closed my eyes as I rinsed my hair. I opened my eyes and looked down, and there was Kesler drinking the water off my penis, like it was a fountain. He's under there with a big shit-eatin' grin, drinking the water as it shoots off the end of my penis. I thought to myself, *If I had a picture of this for his wedding day, his life would be ruined.* I asked him what he was doing, and he said, "I'm drinking the water." I just laughed, but too many dads, I feel, in situations like that would have said, "You can't do that," and make it weird. He was just a kid.

Whatever comes out of your kids' mouths, whatever they do, and whatever you think, remember to roll with it and not make it awkward. If you make it awkward, it'll be difficult for them to come to you later when they have problems because you made the simplest thing awkward in the early stages. Laugh about it because it's only good.

One other example is when my daughter got her period for the first time, which is a big thing for girls. My wife picked her up from school, and Soleil walked into the house out of sorts, cranky, and confused.

She came upstairs and glared at me without saying a word. I asked if she was excited about getting her period, and she said no. Some girls, I went on, get excited because getting their period is a transition to womanhood. She would have none of it. She said it was disgusting and sucked, and her stomach hurt. I said I wasn't going to tell her how to feel, that I just wanted to make sure she was OK. Most dads would have thought, *I ain't talking to her about that. I'm not bringing it up because it's a mom thing*.

I don't want my daughter to think that there's ever a subject or a situation that's off limits with me. I always want to be the person she feels she can come to with a problem, a request, or an awkward situation, and the only way to make sure that happens is to not make things weird in the first place and to keep the lines of communication open.

CHAPTER 11

iPhones Are Not Going Away

You don't want your kids to be zombies, but facts are facts: they will be interacting with technology throughout their lives. Here are some tips for finding that perfect balance.

I'm continually in awe at the speed with which my kids learn and apply technology. To say that their tech skills far exceed mine is an understatement. I feel fortunate that their time at an international school gave them insight into what they're capable of achieving with technology. It was a forward-thinking, tech-savvy school that provided the kids with amazing projects to work on.

One day, Soleil came home and said she had a new project at school using green screen technology. I knew a bit about green screens from our business. We use an app to do some green screen filming in a studio. It's a sophisticated process, and I wondered how they'd do it at school.

A week or two later, she showed me what she'd created. She made a newscast set in Jerusalem at the time of the Crusades, which they were studying in her social studies class. She used the green screen to drop in scenery from the period.

I was blown away and asked her how she'd done it. She explained the process to me and how she'd added sound effects, titles, and subtitles. It was so cool.

I picked my jaw up off the ground. It was an aha moment in which I realized how much technology will be more than just a part of their future: it *is* their future.

CHILDREN AND TECHNOLOGY

I love that teachers are embracing technology. They understand its importance in our children's future. Moving forward, everything our kids will be doing will be impacted by technology. And if they aren't familiar with technology now, they'll have to learn and adapt in the next few years as things continue to develop.

I read an article recently about the future of technology and how it will directly affect our day-to-day lives. It was written by a former law professor, and it blew my mind so much so that I made my two older kids read it, too. In it, he stated that 70 percent of the jobs of today will be obsolete in the next ten years. Even driving our own cars will be a thing of the past, which isn't hard to believe given we already have driverless smart cars. Professionals like lawyers will have less importance as more and more legal advice and templates become available online. Gradually, technology will replace many specialties, so we need to steer our children in the direction of work based in technology.

I must admit that the article scared the shit out of me. It reminded me of Will Smith's movie *I, Robot* in which robots take over people's jobs and then control their lives. I believe that Hollywood sometimes creates movies that are warning signals. They offer insight into what's currently happening or what may happen in the future. (Another Will Smith movie, *Men in Black*, made me think that perhaps we're naïve to think we're the only creatures in the universe. Maybe there are aliens all around us, and the government is trying to soften the blow!) The point is, our children can't avoid technology, and we have to provide them with guidelines so that they stay kids while being able to expand their knowledge of technology to meet the future.

SET LIMITS

I don't advocate giving young kids iPhones, or any phones for that matter. Soleil got a phone when she turned twelve because she'd started babysitting. We wanted her to have a way to communicate with us if a landline wasn't available, like at our house, when she was babysitting. Giving her a cell phone was a safety necessity.

Prior to that, kids don't need a cell phone. Who are they going to call? They see their friends at school every day. If they need to call a buddy, they can use your phone. As far as other types of technology are concerned, there's nothing wrong with young kids using it as long as parents are monitoring how much time they spend on their devices.

Even though I don't want to limit my kids' access to learning and growing with technology, there can be too much of a good thing. Kids can spend too much time on their computers or iPads just like they can in front of the TV. We may be less strict about the amount of time our kids spend on their devices, but we are strict about monitoring technology and continually checking our kids' search histories.

If you don't know how to check a search history, you should definitely learn. The search history keeps track of all the sites anyone who's used the computer or an iPad has visited. Most kids don't know about them, at least not for a while, and it's a good idea not to tell them. They'll figure it out on their own over time. Once they discover where the search history is located, they'll learn how to delete it.

We monitor the search history for signs of misuse. Kids can stumble across stuff that's inappropriate, even if it's an accident. We look for repetitive visits to the same sites that may be bad. We may not be able to be next to our kids every moment they're on the computer, but we can and should know what they're searching and watching.

My boys love YouTube for watching video blogs by gamers on how to play. There are lots of good video gamers who are kid friendly. I'm all for it, especially for Everest, who has a passion for learning to become a gamer. At the same time, there are a lot of wormholes on YouTube to be careful of. One wrong click and your kid can be led down a slippery slope. Kids can end up on a site with bad slang, inappropriate language, or violence. Then that site has to be blocked. It's one reason why we don't let our boys use their computers and iPads in their rooms. It limits our ability to monitor what they're watching.

You'll set yourself up for disaster if you don't scan search histories and make sure that what your kids are watching is appropriate. Parental locks, on the other hand, can be too restrictive and aren't necessarily the best way to manage viewing. Although they can protect kids from seeing things they shouldn't, they also limit access to sites that may be worth exploring, like the History Channel which sometimes contains nudity. While I'm OK with Everest watching videos about tribal life in Africa, for example, where it's normal for women to be topless, I'm not OK with him finding "Big Busty Babes."

It can take time to find what works best in your house. Monitoring your kids' access to sites requires consistency and a commitment, but the payoff is worth it. Your kids will know you're always watching what they're doing, and they'll make better choices because of it. As kids get older, they'll figure out ways to get around a parental lock. If you lock one site, they'll find another, so I'd much rather monitor content and deal with issues that arise with honest questions and answers than have my kids searching for other ways to see what they want.

STAY ON TOP OF LIFE ONLINE

We have a requirement in our house that all passwords and key locks are shared, which some of our friends think is overly strict. Soleil used passwords and key locks on her phone because she doesn't want her brothers going through her stuff, which is fine, but the rule is we know her password.

Aaron and I don't use passwords and key locks, but we do know all the ones our kids use. At any given time, we're able to pick up their phones and check text messages and e-mails. That may seem like an invasion of privacy, which it is, but I don't care. If my kids don't want me to see something on their phone or in their texts, then they shouldn't be doing it or saying it. Whether my kids like it or not, they understand that it's our responsibility as parents to make sure that what they're doing and saying online and with whom is appropriate.

We also remind our kids that whatever they put on the Internet is there to stay, which is something that's hard for any of us to wrap our minds around. What you do, what you say, the pictures you post, everything at some point in time could come back to haunt you. Once you put something into cyberspace, you can't get it back. I have too many friends with teenage girls who send sexy pictures to their boyfriends only to have them shared among hundreds of people. It's devastating for them, but it happens all the time.

We even know one guy who lost his job because of what he posted on Facebook. Our good friend, who was in the financial industry, went to a party with a bunch of other people, also from the financial industry. Everyone got drunk and took some silly pictures. Our friend wasn't doing anything wrong, but he made the mistake of posting the pictures on

Facebook. His employers got wind of it and saw that he was fraternizing with people from the financial industry, and he lost his job.

It sounds extreme, but more and more employers look on Facebook before hiring someone. Seeing a potential employee's social media says a lot about his or her life. If you're not experienced enough with social media to know you can keep your page private, then you could potentially be setting yourself up for disappointment.

Age-appropriate rules apply for computers like they do for TV and other entertainment. What's OK for Soleil and Everest to watch may not always be appropriate for Kesler. Always monitor the maturity level of what your kids are watching. I'm often shocked at what some people let their children watch. Aaron and I went to see the movie *Deadpool*, which was rated R, and there were at least five kids in the theater.

I believe there's a difference between being on the computer and watching television. TV is usually a mindless activity unless it's a knowledge-based program. I much prefer my kids play a game on the computer, even *Minecraft*, because they're at least creating worlds and building villages and castles, even if they're killing zombies in the process. They're using their brains instead of tuning out and passively watching a television program. At the same time, they're developing computer skills that'll serve them moving forward.

BE AWARE OF SOCIAL MEDIA

Soleil still doesn't have a Facebook account because she doesn't need one in my opinion. She doesn't know enough people yet for it to make sense. The people she interacts with she sees at school every day. There's no need to create a Facebook page so that she can randomly post what she happens to be doing.

We did allow her to have an Instagram page, however, so that she can share photos with her friends. Both Aaron and I are on her page so that we can see if what she posts is appropriate. She's been good about what she puts up because she knows we're there, too. Young kids on Facebook are too accessible to predators in my opinion.

Soleil knows she can't friend anyone she doesn't know on her Instagram account. If she's unsure, she comes to us and asks. Young kids can get into trouble if they friend everyone who sends them a friend request. It opens the door to people who prey.

I love my Facebook page. It enables me to communicate

with friends and family all over the world, but I'm mature enough to handle being approached by someone whom I don't know and who wants to join my page. Kids aren't able to make those distinctions, so if you're going to allow your kids to have a social media platform, be sure you monitor it carefully. There are too many sick people out there, and your kids may invite them into their world without understanding the dangers.

I saw an amazing video on YouTube about a young man who did an experiment with social media, and I shared it with Soleil and our friends who have a young daughter. The guy contacted parents and offered to see if their daughter would fall for a social media predator.

The way he did it was by using a fake picture of himself and friending girls on social media, chatting them up, and flirting. After a few days of building up their confidence, he asked them to meet at the park. Every single girl he tested agreed to meet with him, which made me sick to my stomach when I heard about it. They were all good girls and good students from good families, yet they took the bait. The parents who were in on the test were at the park waiting, hiding behind the bushes, and were mortified that their daughter had left home to meet a complete stranger she had known for only a few days online.

In every case, the parents had already had a talk with their daughters about the dangers of social media and not friending people they didn't know. But the girls still decided to meet the guy in the park. One story was particularly amazing. The fellow had invited one girl to go to a party and told her he'd pick her up at 8:00 p.m. at her house. He asked for her address, and she gave it to him. Half an hour before he was supposed to be there, he sent a message saying that he couldn't make it because his car had broken down. His brother would pick her up instead. And this girl got in the car with a guy she didn't know and had never even talked to!

The girl's parents were in the backseat. Her mother was in tears, shocked to discover that her daughter would put herself in that kind of danger. Your daughter could do it, too, even if you think she knows better and would never do something like that. Every parent in the experiment thought that, which is why it's so important to monitor your kids' social media.

LIFE ONLINE VERSUS LIFE IN THE REAL WORLD

We can all get so caught up in our digital life that we forget to be social and spend face-to-face time with our friends. I have a good friend who likes to post pictures of going out to dinner with a group of friends, and when he does, he always seems to catch everyone at the exact moment when they're all looking at their cell phones. It's become a running joke.

It's funny, but it's also sad. We've become so dependent on our devices that we forget to put them away and enjoy one another's company. It's the same with kids. We have to find the balance between allowing our kids to have time on the computer because they're passionate about it and because it develops their computer skills with simply letting them be kids and playing without technology.

At our house, we have break time. During the week when the kids are in school, there's naturally less computer time. After they come home, they have homework and dinner, but on weekends, the kids like to game and do other things online. An hour can quickly turn into many hours if I'm not careful. So we have break time when all the kids turn off their computer and have to find something nondigital to do. Sometimes it takes them a few minutes to disconnect. They wander around in a semidaze, like zombies, trying to figure out what to do next. Then they get into something.

It's rare now that all three of my kids play together because of their age difference. Having eight years between my oldest and my youngest makes it almost impossible to find common ground. One day during break time when the weather was miserable, Everest had the idea to build a fort. He asked to borrow all the sheets and blankets from the guest room, which I agreed to in spite of not looking forward to having to wash everything when they were done. It was well worth the hassle. The three of them spent hours together building a huge fort. They even wanted to eat their lunch inside of it. They completely forgot about their computers for at least three hours. And when they did ask to go back to their computer, they wanted to take one inside the fort and watch a movie together.

It was one of those feel-good, warm-and-fuzzy moments when I realized how glad I was that we have break time. It gives the kids a chance to use their creativity, forces them to interact with one another, and gives them an awesome playtime experience. It's rare that they find common ground, but they had a great time with the fort. It was a wonder-ful moment.

Those opportunities will only happen if we and our kids disconnect from our devices.

Everest's YouTube Presentation

We can't fight technology. It's here to say. Everyone thought TV was going to rot kids' minds when my parents were young. In my generation, it was video games; Super Nintendo was going to ruin every kid's life. Now it's the Internet.

The Internet is a double-edged sword. It's a phenomenal educational and entertainment tool, but it also has some dark sides.

I attended a parent meeting at the kids' school not long ago. Staff were giving us an overview of technology and explaining the rules for using phones and computers at school. They went into issues like the infringement of privacy or what to do when kids abuse their privileges, which was good to know.

I made a point of adding another item for parents to consider: to be sure they have a conversation with their child about the fact that whatever goes on the Internet never goes away. Everything their kids put up, whether it's a picture, a video, or information they send to a friend, will be there forever. Parents have to make that very clear to their kids. Kids may not be concerned about their reputations now, but they will in the future. They have to ask themselves if they'll be comfortable if the whole world sees what they're posting, because the truth is, the whole world will see it.

Years ago, I reserved domain names for my three kids. I own soleilparkinson.com, keslerparkinson.com, and everestparkinson.com. It gives me and my kids the ability to control the first thing someone will see about them.

At the parent meeting, I asked how many people in the room had reserved domain names for their kids. None of them had. They were flabbergasted. I told them they all had to go home and do it right away. They had to think about their children's future. That's what it takes today to be in control as much as possible.

To give an example, I let Everest post his video game reviews on YouTube. One night, he was feeling silly and recorded a video of himself saying over and over again some strange word he picked up from a video game. I told him he was acting like a retard, but he posted it anyway.

His YouTube channel got more hits than it ever had,

something like a thousand hits in forty-eight hours, because he looked like an idiot. People were commenting about how stupid he was.

After a while, Everest started feeling threatened by all the negativity and meanness. I told him there were two things he had to take into account. One was that he had to come to terms with the fact that when he put himself out there, haters would be part of the game. No matter what he chose to post, there'd always be someone who'd hate it. The only thing that mattered was how he chose to deal with the situation when it occurred.

The other thing he had to consider was whether or not he wanted that video to represent him for the rest of his life. Was he proud of the video? He wasn't, so I told him to delete it. He countered with the fact that it had received more than a thousand hits.

I told Everest that it was his choice. I wasn't going to tell him what to do. I just wanted to know if he was proud of the video. I explained that if he wasn't proud of it, he should delete it and learn from the experience. He'd figured out something that had triggered a lot of responses on YouTube. He could learn from that and leverage it in a more positive way in the future. Then he understood and deleted the video.

We're All in This Together

I believe in the adage that says it takes a village to raise a child. Especially as mothers, we don't always ask for help because of pride. We worry that we'll be judged, don't have our shit together, and are unable to manage our homes.

That's unfortunate. Many cultures rely on the larger family to raise their children, though it's not the North American way. We're so dead set on doing everything ourselves and proving to others that we can do it alone.

My friends know that I want them to treat my children as their own. If we were at a friend's house and my children were doing something inappropriate, I'd want them to correct my kids, and vice versa. Together, we raise great kids. I have a close group of friends with kids ranging from ages one to sixteen, and we all take responsibility for one another's children. We hang out together, play together, and go camping together, and none of us wants to be surrounded by kids who are assholes. We all take responsibility so that we can enjoy one another's company. Together, we're creating healthy, positive, smart, and well-adjusted children.

Because both Aaron and I were adventurous and difficult as teenagers, we joke with Soleil and tell her that there isn't anything that she'll do that we haven't already done ourselves. There's no lie or deception, we say, that we haven't used, which may not be 100 percent true.

Aaron likes to tell the story about when he was seventeen and missed curfew. In his house, missing curfew was the one thing for which there was no exception. His parents would get ridiculously angry if he came in late and woke everyone up because he had a little sister who was eight years younger than him, and both his parents had to be at work early.

If he missed curfew, the doors were locked and he had to figure things out on his own. One Christmas Eve, he was out with his buddies and came home late. His parents had locked the door. He normally had a key to the back door, which led into the basement and was fine to use. However, this time he had left his keys at his friend's house.

He knew that the worst thing he could do was to knock on the door or ring the doorbell, so he decided to sleep in the sauna. They had a big pool and an outdoor sauna in the backyard. Because they never used the sauna, his dad, who was a beverage rep, used to store cases of Snapple in it.

Aaron decided he'd turn on the sauna to warm things up because it was December and cold, and he made himself a bed on top of the Snapple boxes. When he woke up the next morning, the heat in the sauna was so dry that he had to peel his eyes open. He was dehydrated and because the air was so thick inside the sauna, he had to suck in to breathe.

Steaming, he threw open the door to the backyard, leaped out, and jumped into the freezing-cold swimming pool. When he looked up, he saw his mom, dad, and little sister looking out the kitchen window. His parents were shaking their heads as if to say, "You idiot," but they weren't mad at him. As stupid as it was and as crazy as he had been to jump in the pool, they couldn't be mad at him because he'd followed the rules. He'd taken responsibility for his actions, slept in the sauna, and didn't wake anyone. The fact that he nearly died of dehydration sleeping on top of a pile of Snapple was a different problem!

We've all done stupid things, so we have to be able to cut our kids a bit of slack and realize that they'll do stupid things, too, despite all our good parenting and guidance. They'll test us the same way we tested our parents. We have to do our best to be patient with them and navigate each situation.

At some point, I know Soleil will think she's smarter than us. She'll try to trick us, and we won't figure it out. It's part of growing up. It's a process of trial and error for everyone— for our kids about what they can get away with and for us on how to parent.

You'll make mistakes. Sometimes your parenting techniques will work, and at other times they'll fail terribly. My kids are far from perfect. They still misbehave and can be little assholes, but 95 percent of the time, they're great kids. If the same is true for your kids, you're doing a really good job.

When my kids go to my mom's house and they're being great kids, I know the basics are in place, such as having good manners, saying please and thank you, being quiet, and behaving appropriately. A lot of parenting is figuring things out as you go. It may not always look like you know what you're doing.

Remember that putting in the time up front will save you down the line. Parenting can be a grind, especially at the beginning. There will be days when it feels endless and there are no rewards, days with lots of tears, and days of missing being single. That's natural. But if you don't consistently put in the effort at the beginning when your kids are young and impressionable, you'll be picking them up from juvenile hall. Then the damage is irreversible. Creating positive, happy children takes work, but it's worth it. When I leave this earth, I want to know my children aren't being assholes.

I hope that if they choose to have children of their own, they'll take what they learned from Aaron and me to create the next generation of nonasshole kids. That's how it works. We should all try to be better parents than our parents were. That's how we create a better world.

If we do just enough parenting to get by, we'll get mediocre children. And mediocre kids who lack a solid good base become mediocre adults who don't inspire, grow, or pass on those things that will create a next great generation.

We can't expect the next generation to be better if we don't teach them a better way. I hope we're teaching our kids a better way to accept, love, and be good people. At the end of the day, it doesn't matter what your career is or how you choose to spend your time if you're not fundamentally a good person.

One day, our children may have to take care of us, and hopefully, we've been good parents and provided them with a foundation of respect so that it's not going to be a chore for them. If we've done a good job, they'll want to take care of us as we get older. If not, we'll be in trouble. They'll drop us off on the doorstep of a nursing home, pay the monthly bill, and never come to see us. I certainly don't want that from my children.

Our kids are always going to have moments when they misbehave and embarrass us. There will be times when you think your kid is being an asshole. Those times will always happen because your kids are constantly growing, learning, and testing. It's how you respond that will prevent the bad behavior from becoming a habit. Take advantage of bad behavior and turn it into a teachable moment so that it never happens again!

Every situation, good or bad, has the potential for being a teachable moment. Never overlook when your kids are being bad because it's inconvenient or when they're good, which merits recognition, and don't get caught up in parenting from only the negative. Parenting from the positive will create fabulous kids even faster!

About the Author

LIZ PARKINSON is the mother of three great kids, who light up her life and test her character on a daily basis, and author of the Ronnie Rhino children's books, an Amazon best seller.

She and her husband, Aaron, currently own an online nutrition and fitness support program that guides its 500,000-plus members in making one small change a day. Prior to being a fitness coach, Liz owned a wedding floral business, managed several restaurants, and was a nightclub bartender.

Her goal in parenting is to raise children who as adults don't take thirty years to recover from their childhood and blame her as the reason they turned out to be total assholes.

For more about Liz, visit www.lizandkids.com.